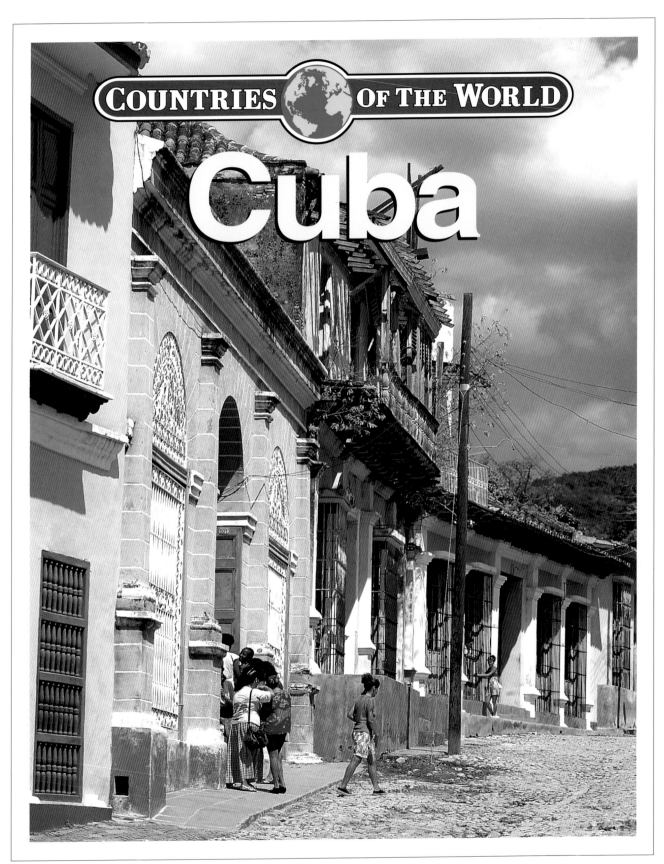

COUNTRIES OF THE WORLD

Cuba

Gareth Stevens Publishing
MILWAUKEE

About the Author: Mark Cramer is a freelance writer and teacher based in Bolivia. A New Yorker with a mind to travel, he has published books on Bolivia, Cuba, Mexico, and various parts of the United States.

Written by
MARK CRAMER

Edited by
KEN CHANG

Designed by
LYNN CHIN

Picture research by
SUSAN JANE MANUEL

First published in North America in 2000 by
Gareth Stevens Publishing
1555 North RiverCenter Drive, Suite 201
Milwaukee, Wisconsin 53212 USA

For a free color catalog describing
Gareth Stevens' list of high-quality books
and multimedia programs, call
1-800-542-2595 (USA) or
1-800-461-9120 (CANADA).
Gareth Stevens Publishing's
Fax: (414) 225-0377.

© **TIMES EDITIONS PTE LTD 2000**
Originated and designed by
Times Editions Pte Ltd
Times Centre, 1 New Industrial Road
Singapore 536196
http://www.timesone.com.sg/te

Library of Congress Cataloging-in-Publication Data
Cramer, Mark
Cuba / by Mark Cramer.
p.   cm. -- (Countries of the world)
Includes bibliographical references and index.
Summary: Introduces the geography, history, economy, government, culture, food, and people of Cuba.
ISBN 0-8368-2316-8 (lib. bdg.)
1. Cuba--Juvenile literature. [1. Cuba.] I. Title.
II. Series: Countries of the world (Milwaukee, Wis.)
F1758.5.C73   2000
972.91--dc21   99-33353

Printed in Malaysia

1 2 3 4 5 6 7 8 9 04 03 02 01 00

PICTURE CREDITS
A.N.A. Press Agency: 4, 5, 31, 37
Archive Photos: 15 (bottom), 45, 70, 72, 78 (bottom), 84 (both), 85
Canadian High Commission: 80
Mark Cramer: 90
John Denham: 35
Focus Team-Italy: 77
HBL Network Photo Agency: 13, 15 (center), 17 (both), 18 (both), 21, 41, 48, 53, 54, 56, 71, 83
Hutchison Library: 23, 52, 69 (bottom)
International Photobank: Cover, 1, 2, 16, 33, 49 (top)
Bjorn Klingwall: 8, 19, 24, 25, 29, 32, 65
Earl and Nazima Kowall: 3 (top), 38, 78 (top)
North Wind Picture Archives: 10, 11 (both), 62
Christine Osborne: 7, 26, 28, 40, 46, 49 (bottom), 58, 60, 61
David Simson: 9 (top), 20, 30, 44, 55, 63, 66, 81, 91
South American Pictures: 3 (bottom), 6, 9 (bottom), 12, 15 (top), 22, 27, 34, 36, 39, 42, 43, 47, 50, 51, 57, 64, 67, 68, 73, 74
Liba Taylor: 14, 75
Vision Photo Agency: 79
Nik Wheeler: 3 (center), 59, 69 (top), 76, 82

Digital Scanning by Superskill Graphics Pte Ltd

Contents

4

AN OVERVIEW OF CUBA

Over the last century, the Republic of Cuba has been one of the most controversial countries in the world — first as a rebellious, upstart nation occupied by the U.S. military, and then as a pro-Soviet, socialist state under Fidel Castro. Around the world, Cuba is often known more for its politics (especially its stormy relations with the United States) than for its unique culture, its history, or its position at the forefront of Latin America. The real story of Cuba begins with the land and how it has shaped the Cuban people's heritage. Although Cuba has been one of the most isolated countries in Latin America since 1959, its citizens are still thriving intellectually, artistically, and spiritually.

Opposite: **A huge crowd of Cubans gathers in Havana's Plaza de Revolución for a political rally.**

Below: **In Havana, patriotic Cubans assemble at the José Martí memorial to celebrate the anniversary of the national rebellion led by Fidel Castro in 1953.**

THE FLAG OF CUBA

Although not officially adopted until 1898, the Cuban flag dates back to 1850, when Narciso López, a Spanish-Venezuelan, tried, unsuccessfully, to liberate Cuba from Spain and annex it to the United States. López had designed a Cuban national flag featuring a red triangle (its three sides representing liberty, equality, and fraternity, and its color symbolizing revolutionary bloodshed) and a single white star (which he hoped to add to the other stars of the U.S. flag). In 1851, López returned to Cuba from U.S. exile to start a new revolution, but he was quickly defeated by the Spaniards. López's revolutionary passion lives on in the Cuban flag.

Geography

The Republic of Cuba is spread out over an archipelago of 1,600 islands and islets. Most of the population lives on the island of Cuba itself, which has 3,570 miles (5,744 kilometers) of coastline and an area of 40,519 square miles (104,944 square km), making it the fifteenth largest island in the world. The Cuban archipelago actually forms part of the Antilles, a much longer island chain that stretches east to west and marks the northern edge of the Caribbean Sea. Within the Cuban archipelago are five smaller island chains: the Los Colorados, the Sabana, the Camagüey, the Jardines de la Reina, and the Los Canarreos — all of which feature vast beaches, hidden coves and inlets, and beautiful coral reefs.

Cuba lies at the crossroads of North America, Central America, the Gulf of Mexico, the Caribbean Sea, and the Atlantic Ocean. The island's immediate neighbors include Haiti, just 48 miles (77 km) to the east; Mexico, 120 miles (193 km) to the west; Florida and the Bahamas, about 90 miles (145 km) to the north; and Jamaica, 87 miles (140 km) to the south.

Below: **The small island of Cayo Largo is famous for its picturesque beaches and numerous tourist resorts. Cayo Largo is one of many islands in the Canarreos Archipelago, which runs along the southwestern coast of Cuba.**

Cuba is famous for its beaches, but rural Cubans, called *guajiros* (gwa-HEE-rohs), prefer the rugged green mountains of the interior. The island of Cuba has three important mountain ranges. The peculiar Sierra de los Órganos cuts through the tobacco-growing province of Pinar del Río in western Cuba. These mountains are shaped in distinctive, flat-topped outcrops called *mogotes* (moh-GOH-tehs), which are unlike any other mountains in the world. The central range, the Sierra de Trinidad, rises to 3,793 feet (1,156 meters) at San Juan Peak and roughly divides Cuba in half. Running parallel with the southeastern coast is the famous Sierra Maestra, where Fidel Castro's revolutionary army waged its guerrilla war during the late 1950s. The Sierra Maestra's highest peak, the magnificent Pico Turquino, climbs to 6,561 feet (2,000 m).

The longest river in Cuba, the Cauto, springs from the Sierra Maestra and flows west for 230 miles (370 km) before emptying into the Gulf of Guacanayabo. The rugged terrain forces many of Cuba's 600 rivers to drop into waterfalls, carving out refreshing swimming holes where many Cubans cool off in the summer.

Above: **The Sierra Maestra is the longest mountain range in Cuba, stretching more than 100 miles (161 km) across the provinces of Granma and Santiago de Cuba. Visitors can reach the summit of Pico Turquino, the highest point in Cuba, after about six hours of hiking and climbing.**

MOGOTES

Mogotes are spectacular geological formations unique to Cuba. Over the years, they have attracted the attention of scientists, spelunkers, mountaineers, artists, and even disco lovers.
(A Closer Look, page 56)

Climate and Seasons

Cuba has a tropical climate that is cooled by westerly trade winds; the annual mean temperature is 75° Fahrenheit (24° Celsius), which is cooler than most tropical countries. Cuba has only two seasons during the year: the wet season, which lasts from May through October, and the dry season, which starts in November and lasts through April. In January, the coolest month, temperatures range from 56° to 70° F (13° to 21° C); in August, summer temperatures average 82° F (28° C), and the humidity hovers at 80 percent. A tropical hurricane hits Cuba every one to two years, during the wet season.

Plants and Animals

The 8,000 tropical plant species in Cuba thrive in a very limited space, since most of the island's flat or forested areas have been turned into tobacco, coffee, or sugar plantations. Cuba's sixty palm tree species include the fan-leafed Washingtonia and the towering royal palm — Cuba's national tree — which can grow as high as 75 feet (23 m). The banyan tree is a favorite of shade-seekers during the hot Cuban summer. Native flowers include the butterfly jasmine and various orchids.

Above: **The unusual Washingtonia palm is a common sight in Cuba. The tree retains all its dead leaves, which form a bushy, cylindrical "skirt" that completely hides the trunk.**

Cuba is famous for its eclectic variety of animal species, including tarantulas, iguanas, sharks, bats, and flamingos. Some of Cuba's rarest wildlife species find refuge in a swampy area southwest of Havana called Ciénega de Zapata (Zapata Marsh). Among the swamp's animal celebrities are the *majá* (ma-HAH), a nonpoisonous, nocturnal python; the 10-foot (3-m)-long alligator gar, one of the largest freshwater fishes in the world; and the gentle, slow-moving manatee, or sea cow. The *jutía* (hoo-TEE-ah), or tree-rat, is an unusual, native mammal species whose gamey meat suits many Cubans' tastes.

More than 300 bird species can be found in Cuba, including the tocororo, whose red, white, and blue feathers match the colors of the Cuban flag. The tiny bee hummingbird, just 0.5 inch (1.3 centimeters) long, is the smallest bird in the world, and its wings move faster than those of any animal known to man. The long-necked white heron protects Cuba's cattle industry by eating deadly parasites from cows' skin. In the countryside, each cow is dutifully accompanied by its "assigned" white heron.

Above: The tropical river crab is a rare freshwater creature that can breathe both underwater and on land. These crabs can be found in soggy marshlands, such as Ciénega de Zapata in western Cuba.

Left: A Cuban ground iguana delights a trio of tourists. An adult ground iguana reaches a length of 4 feet (1.2 m) and is a surprisingly quick mover. Unfortunately, dogs and cats brought in by foreign settlers have greatly reduced its numbers.

History

Little is known about Cuba's original native people, the Taino and Ciboney Indians, except that they became extinct less than a hundred years after Christopher Columbus discovered Cuba for Spain in 1492. Epidemic diseases, brutality, and forced labor brought on by the Spanish colonists quickly wiped out these peaceful tribes. During the 1600s, Cuba became a popular target for European pirates who looted not only Spanish ships but also entire cities. Yet Spain refused to let go of the island because it remained a strategic platform for trade, smuggling, Christian missionaries, and further military conquests in the Americas.

In the 1700s, the Spanish government turned Cuba into an agricultural powerhouse by importing African slaves to work on colonial sugar plantations. Spanish landowners quickly became the wealthy elites of Cuban society, while creoles (Spaniards born in Cuba), mulattoes (mixed Spanish-Africans), free blacks, and black slaves suffered from the harsh unfairness of Spanish rule.

PIRATES

For hundreds of years, ruthless pirates made Cuba a danger zone for merchants and sailors. Massive fortresses tower over many of the island's coastal cities.

(A Closer Look, page 62)

Below: **During the eighteenth century, Havana Bay became one of the busiest harbors in Spain's colonial empire.**

Left: The USS *Indiana* was part of a strong naval squadron used against the Spanish fleet in the Battle of Santiago, the last major battle of the Spanish-American War. Spain surrendered Santiago de Cuba to the United States on July 17, 1898, signaling the end of the war.

Wars of Independence

In 1868, Carlos Manuel de Céspedes, a white landowner, freed his slaves and launched a rebellion against Spain. Máximo Gómez, a black exile from Santo Domingo, and Antonio Maceo, a Cuban mulatto, continued the independence movement through 1878 despite dwindling support. Slavery was officially abolished in 1886, but blacks were given few economic opportunities.

In 1895, Cuban exile José Martí joined Maceo and Gómez to engage the Spaniards in a second war of independence. This conflict escalated into the Spanish-American War after the U.S. battleship *Maine* mysteriously exploded in Havana Bay on February 15, 1898, killing 260 U.S. sailors. The Spaniards claimed the explosion was an accident, but the U.S. government regarded it as an act of aggression and declared war. The Spanish-American War, fought in both the Caribbean and in the Philippines, lasted only four months, with the U.S. Navy garnering victories on both fronts. Spain granted Cuba its independence on December 10, 1898, but the U.S. military remained to oversee the new republic.

Above: In 1898, Theodore Roosevelt commanded the 1st Volunteer Cavalry (known as "the Rough Riders"), which fought bravely in Cuba during the Spanish-American War. Roosevelt became President of the United States in 1901.

U.S. Occupation and Cuban Discontent

Despite its official independence, Cuba endured two years of U.S. military occupation before the first elected president of Cuba, Tomás Estrada Palma, took office in 1902. In order to end the U.S. occupation, however, Cuba had to adopt the Platt Amendment, which legally permitted U.S. intervention in Cuba's political and economic affairs. The Platt Amendment also allowed the United States to establish the Guantánamo Naval Base, which was built in 1903 and still operates today.

From 1902 to 1959, U.S. businesses owned most of Cuba's farms and industries. Meanwhile, the repressive regimes of Cuban dictators, such as Gerardo Machado (1925–1933) and Fulgencio Batista (1933–1944, 1952–1959), left a trail of political corruption, poverty, and military brutality. In 1952, Batista, who had retired from politics in 1944, abruptly returned to power by overthrowing the government and canceling the national elections. For Fidel Castro, a lawyer from Havana who had been on the legislative ballot, the seeds of revolution had been sown.

Above: **Built in 1922, the Presidential Palace stands tall in central Havana. After Fidel Castro overthrew the corrupt Batista regime in 1959, the regal palace was converted into the Museum of the Revolution.**

The Rise and Revolution of Fidel Castro

On July 26, 1953, Castro and a small army of rebels attacked the Moncada military base in the province of Santiago de Cuba. Most of the rebels were massacred by Batista's army, and Castro was arrested, tried, and sentenced to a prison term of fifteen years.

Upon his early release from prison in 1955, Castro, along with his brother Raúl and Argentine revolutionary Ernesto "Che" Guevara, assembled a new rebel group of Cuban exiles in Mexico. Named the *26th of July Movement*, the group first struck in 1956, when Castro landed off the coast of Granma with an army of eighty-one men. The rebels were defeated badly in their first battle, but the dozen survivors managed to round up enough popular support and volunteer soldiers to wage a successful guerrilla campaign in the highlands of the Sierra Maestra. Within two years, Castro commanded a strong army of 800 men that consistently defended its position against Batista's army of 30,000. Batista panicked and fled Cuba on January 1, 1959. The revolutionary army, led by Che Guevera and Camilo Cienfuegos, entered Havana triumphantly the next day. Castro became premier and head of the government of Cuba in February 1959.

CHE GUEVARA

Ernesto "Che" Guevara was a trusted military and political advisor to Fidel Castro for more than a decade. A scholar, doctor, writer, orator, communist, guerrilla leader, and revolutionary hero, Guevara was an idealistic warrior who hoped to liberate Latin America from poverty and elitist political regimes.
(A Closer Look, page 52)

Left: Fidel Castro led his revolutionary army to victory in 1959, a pivotal year in Cuban history. Once in power, Castro nationalized all Cuban farms and industries, established free health care and free education, and adopted a pro-Soviet foreign policy.

The Modern Socialist Republic

In 1959, Castro started a series of radical socialist measures that were heard around the world. An alarmed United States (and an intrigued Soviet Union) paid close attention as Cuba's new government nationalized all foreign-owned properties and businesses, outlawed political parties, and tried to spread its revolution to other Latin American countries, such as Bolivia and Venezuela. By 1962, the U.S. government had broken all ties with Cuba, financed a disastrous invasion of Cuba by Cuban exiles, and failed in repeated attempts to assassinate Castro. In contrast, the Soviets supported Castro's regime by buying Cuban sugar (Cuba's main export) and supplying weapons — including nuclear missiles that could target U.S. cities. To resolve the tense Cuban missile crisis of 1962, the United States agreed not to invade Cuba, and the Soviet Union removed its missiles from Cuba.

In 1991, the Soviet Union collapsed, and Cuba's dependent economy collapsed with it. Castro declared a "special period in a time of peace," during which he expected Cubans to patriotically cope with the hard times ahead.

THE BALSEROS

After Cuba lost its Soviet lifeline in 1991, a handful of impoverished Cubans fled the country using whatever means necessary. Some of these refugees, called *balseros* (bahl-SEH-rohs), tried to sail across the Straits of Florida to the United States in makeshift rafts.

Below: A crowd of young Cubans celebrates the anniversary of the revolution of 1959. Through both triumphs and hardships, Cubans have shown a great deal of national pride.

José Martí (1853–1895)

One of Cuba's most inspirational national heroes, José Martí led the movement for Cuban independence in the late 1800s. Exiled to Spain in 1871 for publishing his liberal views in his newspaper *The Free Fatherland*, Martí earned his law degree and, over the next twenty years, attracted international recognition as a newspaper columnist, political commentator, poet, libertarian, and patriot-in-exile. In 1895, he returned to Cuba to fight against the Spaniards in the second war of independence. Although Martí died in battle, his revolution continued, and Cuba became independent from Spain in 1898.

José Martí

Fidel Castro (c. 1926–)

Fidel Castro, one of the most important revolutionaries in world history, has been the head of Cuba's government since 1959. Despite stormy Cuba-U.S. relations and the 1991 breakup of the Soviet Union (which had supported Cuba for thirty years), Castro has remained firmly in control of the country. He has recently allowed for some capitalist reforms in Cuba and released a number of political prisoners, but he vows to defend socialism and the integrity of his regime.

Fidel Castro

Nicolás Guillén (1902–1989)

Regarded as Cuba's national poet, Nicolás Guillén was not only a writer but also a social protest leader who championed equal rights. The Afro-Cuban Guillén was a close friend of African-American poet Langston Hughes, and these two literary greats often translated each other's work. After being exiled from Cuba during the Batista regime, Guillén was welcomed back in 1959 to serve as the director of Cuba's Union of Writers and Artists.

María Caridad Colón (1959–)

Olympian María Caridad Colón represents a generation of Cuban women who have achieved greatness under the socialist government's support for women's rights. As a youth, Colón broke the Latin American record for the longest javelin toss. At the 1980 Olympic Games, Colón became the first woman from a developing country to win an Olympic gold medal.

Nicolás Guillén

15

Government and the Economy

Cuba is a socialist republic. The government controls the means of the economy, and the citizens are empowered by their vote to elect representatives in government. The president is the head of state and the commander in chief of the armed forces. In 1976, Cuba adopted a new constitution that established the current structure of the government, which has since been dominated by the Communist Party of Cuba and President Fidel Castro. Government powers are split between the executive State Council and the legislative "Organs of People's Power."

The Communist Party of Cuba

In 1959, Castro's revolutionaries dissolved all political parties in Cuba in favor of a one-party system. Six years later, the Communist Party of Cuba was established as the official national political party. Castro was named the party's first secretary in 1976.

EARNING VOTES

Cuban politics is based on regional and local public forums that do not have corporate sponsors. This differs greatly from politics in North America, where powerful organizations can influence government decisions by contributing campaign money.

Below: **The former National Capitol building in Havana now serves as the main office for the Cuban Academy of Sciences.**

Organs of People's Power

The National Assembly of the People's Power consists of 589 members who represent 169 municipalities. Elected directly by the people, the delegates of the National Assembly meet twice a year for lawmaking proceedings; they also elect the thirty-one members of the State Council, including the president.

Cuba is divided into fourteen official provinces, each of which has its own provincial assembly of elected delegates. Cities, city districts, and even neighborhoods also have their own local assemblies. The structure of these "Organs" is designed to foster all people's participation in the political process.

The State Council and President

The power of Cuba's political system is centralized in the State Council, which enforces law and public policy. The president oversees the State Council and also appoints a Council of Ministers to advise him in administrative matters. Fidel Castro was appointed president of the State Council in 1976 and continues to serve in this office today.

Mass Organizations

The Cuban government created several mass organizations to deal with social and welfare issues. These agencies include the Confederation of Cuban Workers, the Federation of Cuban Women, and the Committees for the Defense of the Revolution.

PARTY PLAYERS

The Communist Party is the legal political party in Cuba. At the top of the party's chain of command is the Secretariat, headed by Fidel and Raúl Castro. The Secretariat directs the 225-member Central Committee, which is elected by regional and local party members.

Above: **A Havana mural depicts Camilo Cienfuegos** *(left)* **and Che Guevara** *(right)*, **leaders of the revolution that established Cuba's modern government.**

Left: A farmer follows his cattle-drawn wagon down a dirt road in Viñales, a small town in western Cuba known for its fertile tobacco fields.

A Newly Independent Economy

After the 1991 Soviet breakup, Cuba suddenly lost its primary trading partner and 40 percent of its economy. As Cuba's "special period" continues today, Cubans regularly endure severe food, fuel, and medicine shortages. In 1996, the United States aggravated these hardships by tightening its embargo against Cuba. For the country to survive, Castro had to accelerate certain capitalist reforms (which had been initiated in the 1980s), such as permitting the use of U.S. dollars and encouraging foreign investment.

Working for the State

In a socialist state, the people work for the collective good of the community, not for individual profit. In Cuba, laborers earn nearly as much as professionals, and, in some cases, even more. A taxi driver, for example, may earn more than a doctor. With too many professionals in the national work force, the Cuban government sends many doctors and scientists abroad to help other countries. Farmers, miners, factory workers, and fishermen make up most of the domestic work force. Many Cubans also work in education, tourism, performing arts, athletics, and medicine.

CIGARS

Hand-rolled, finely crafted Cuban cigars are the best in the world. Many foreigners think of Cuban cigars as flashy luxury items or clichéd props for Hollywood actors. But, for Cubans, the cigar is a national tradition and pastime.

(A Closer Look, page 48)

Agriculture, Industry, and Trade

Cuban agriculture, still dominated by sugarcane farms, is slowly diversifying despite the tropical climate. Other cash crops in Cuba include bananas, citrus fruits, tobacco, and coffee.

Tourism, the fastest growing industry in Cuba, is not restricted to beach resorts. Havana is a magnet for international professional conferences, especially in the fields of medicine and education. The service industry is also expanding, as Cuban entrepreneurs open up new restaurants, repair shops, and other small businesses.

Cuba exports sugar, minerals, cigars, pharmaceuticals, and food products. Major imports include fossil fuels, rice, and cotton. Cuba's major trading partners are Canada, Spain, and Mexico.

Partially Free Enterprise

Cuba now permits private businesses, but with restrictions to prevent some people from becoming more privileged than others. Business owners must do their own work, hire no employees, and pay heavy taxes. Cuba is evolving toward a "mixed economy," with socialism coexisting with free-market capitalism.

ORGANIC RESCUE

In 1991, thirty years of Soviet economic aid to Cuba came to an end, leaving the Cuban economy in shambles. Agriculture was hit the hardest, as the Cuban government could no longer afford to buy fertilizers and pesticides for farmers. Scientists saved Cuba from famine by using organic, not chemical, methods.
(A Closer Look, page 60)

Below: Nickel is Cuba's most important mining export. This nickel smelting plant operates in Moa, a city on the eastern coast of Cuba.

People and Lifestyle

Before 1959, Cuban society was sharply segregated by both race and gender. Even the dictator Fulgencio Batista was excluded from the all-white Havana Yacht Club because he was mulatto. Women were excluded from many professions and expected to handle only household duties. After the 1959 revolution, the Cuban government declared racism and sexism illegal. Modern Cuba is now a land of opportunity for women and ethnic minorities.

Another major achievement of the revolution was nationalizing education so that all Cuban children had equal access to quality schooling. Government programs focused on rural areas to eliminate urban-class privileges and other socioeconomic differences. Stripped of their rank, most white upper-class Cubans left their country shortly after the revolution; the people who remained inherited a completely restructured society. With capitalism gone, Cuban citizens channeled their ambitions into education and athletics instead of making money.

RACE RELATIONS

Since 1959, Cuba has forged a progressive government policy to eliminate racial discrimination. Today, Cuba is one of the most racially integrated societies in the world.
(*A Closer Look*, page 64)

Left: Three boys relax in the colorful streets of Havana. In Cuba, opportunities for education, jobs, and friendships do not depend on race or gender.

Ethnic Groups, Not Ethnic Classes

Cuba's main ethnic groups are whites, blacks, and mixed races (mulattoes and mestizos, or people of mixed Spanish and native Indian ancestry). Mixed races and blacks account for more than half the population and occupy the same proportion of professional jobs as whites — a great achievement considering the long history of racism in Cuba. The main ethnic minority groups are the Chinese and the Jews, who combine to form less than 1 percent of the population. Although many Chinese fled Cuba after the 1959 revolution, Havana's Chinatown is still a thriving area. Cuban Jews have seen their religious needs formally addressed by the government. When private businesses were outlawed shortly after the revolution, Castro made an exception for Jewish meat merchants so that traditional Jews could obtain kosher foods.

Cuba's classless society is now threatened by the U.S. dollar, which discriminates against Cubans who earn only Cuban pesos. Cubans receiving U.S. dollars from tourism-related jobs or from abroad are emerging as a privileged new social class. The government hopes to restore equality by taxing dollar income.

Above: A Cuban woman stands outside her home in Trinidad, a city on the coast of southern central Cuba. Like other Cuban cities, Trinidad has a multiethnic heritage (Spanish, West African, and native Indian) that is reflected in the traditions, languages, and faces of its people.

Family Life

Cuban families, like typical Latin American families, are marked by strong ties among extended family members and children's devoted respect toward their elders. Despite these traditional similarities, visitors from more conservative regions of Latin America are often impressed by the friendly informality between Cuban children and their parents.

Another important difference between Cuban families and other Latin American families is that Cuban women have been fully liberated from the traditional pressures to stay at home. The era of modern Cuban women began with the 1959 revolution, which advocated an equal opportunity workplace for men and women. Today, working women make up 42 percent of Cuba's

Below: In both urban and rural communities, Cuba is an integrated, multicultural society. These young guajiros live in the Sierra de los Órganos.

national labor force, as well as 22 percent of Cuba's congressional representatives — easily the highest figures in Latin America. Another effect of Cuba's equal rights reforms was a dramatic increase in the national divorce rate, which is now one of the highest in the world. Yet most Cuban families have adapted well to the government's promotion of women's rights and how it has changed roles within the family unit. With mothers so active and ambitious, Cuban fathers and children have learned to help out at home. In many households, chores and responsibilities are shared between all family members.

COMMUNITY

In many ways, community is just an extension of the family in Cuba. Cubans have always nurtured a neighborhood-oriented mentality. Even city residents feel like small-town folks, tightly bonded to their local community.
(A Closer Look, page 50)

The average Cuban mother has only 1.9 children, one of the lowest birth rates in Latin America. Although the Cuban nuclear family tends to be small, it is enriched by a caring network of relatives, neighbors, and friends. The Cuban concept of family never remains confined to the home; different families living in the same neighborhood often treat each other like blood relatives. When one family has financial or personal problems, the surrounding families offer their support. Cubans often leave their apartment front doors open, expecting informal visits from neighbors and relatives.

Living space is a prized possession in Cuba. Most Cubans live in small, cramped apartments that offer little privacy to any of the family members. But a lack of living space is a small price

WOMEN OF THE REVOLUTION

Nowhere in the world have women been as active politically, economically, and culturally than in Cuba. Cuban women have been some of the most enthusiastic supporters of Fidel Castro's socialist revolution.

(A Closer Look, page 72)

Above: **Three women enjoy the casual, open atmosphere of downtown Havana.**

to pay for the privileges entitled to every Cuban: free health care, free child care, and free education. These privileges relieve the family of a lot of financial and emotional strain and make it easier to live in such close quarters. Young adults usually live with their parents until they get married, but they have many opportunities to leave the house for extended periods of time. Teenagers can join the youth brigades, which venture into the countryside and help out local farmers; students of various ages can go on school-sponsored field trips to wilderness retreats called *campismos* (cahm-PEES-mos) for some fun outdoor recreation.

Education

In 1959, more than one million Cuban adults could not read or write. Speaking to the United Nations in 1961, Fidel Castro promised he would increase Cuba's literacy to over 90 percent (from 60 percent in 1959) within a year. To meet this challenge, the government sent teachers, workers, and teenagers to all areas of Cuba to teach people how to read. The program was a dramatic success. Today, Cuba's literacy rate stands at 96 percent.

The Cuban government has also focused on reforming the nation's schools, which were once known for widely uneven standards as well as discrimination (women and blacks usually received poorer educations than men and whites). In 1961, the government abolished private schools and organized a free and equal national education system for all Cubans. Women and blacks have since achieved equal representation in most professions. In addition, Cuba has developed into the academic hub of Latin America and a leader in scientific research.

Education begins in day-care centers, which accept children from the age of forty-five days to six years old. Children receive meals and are taught simple skills to prepare them for reading,

Left: **The headmaster of an urban high school prepares for a class.**

mathematics, and science subjects. After a year of kindergarten, children begin elementary school, which lasts from first through sixth grade. Spanish and math are the most important subjects, and teachers emphasize good study habits. Junior high school (seventh through ninth grade) and high school (tenth through twelfth grade) focus on technical and professional skills and foster a competitive learning environment. High school students are required to take courses in history, mathematics, biology, chemistry, and physics, and they have little room in their schedules for elective courses. University-level education is free, but high school students must achieve very high grades to gain admission.

In the post-Soviet 1990s, Cuba's educational system has struggled to maintain its high standards. Government funding is tight, and schools need more money to pay for teaching staff, libraries, and classrooms. Teaching shortages are particularly acute in music and art subjects. Despite their modest budgets, Cuban schools manage to offer an exciting program of extracurricular activities, including overnight trips, sports, dances, festivals, and volunteer work. Youngsters contribute one Cuban peso (1 CUP), or U.S. $0.04, every month in fees for after-school activities.

Above: Schoolgirls take a break from class at the Lenin School in Havana. The Cuban educational system focuses on many practical and technical skills that enable students to quickly find work. Many students are able to find useful jobs while still in school.

Religion

Latin America is often associated with Roman Catholicism, but Cuba is a major exception. During the sixteenth century, Spanish Catholic missionaries were unable to convert many of the native Cuban Indians simply because the Indians were being wiped out by disease and slavery on colonial plantations. As African slaves were brought to Cuba, they identified the Catholic Church with the abuses of Spanish colonialism and generally rejected Christianity. Blacks and mulattoes (even those who converted to the Catholic church) kept their faith in African saints, while Cuban whites continued to practice Catholicism.

Since Christian slave owners forbade the practice of pagan religions, many slaves disguised their worship of African gods as worship of Christian saints. This practice gradually evolved into Santería, a unique Afro-Cuban religion that combines West African religious culture with Roman Catholicism. Santerían saints, called *orishas* (oh-REE-shahs), include *Yemanyá* (yeh-mahn-YAH), the goddess of the seas, who, during colonial

Above: **The Cathedral San Cristobal de la Habana was built between 1704 and 1777 by the Catholic church. The bustling plaza in front of the cathedral is one of the most popular gathering places in Havana.**

times, was disguised as the Blessed Virgin Mary; *Changó* (chahn-GOH), the god of fire, who wears red and controls lightning from the tops of palm trees; and *Obatalá* (oh-bah-tah-LAH), who is dressed in white and associated with Christ. Today, there are at least 4,000 Santerían priests, or *babalawos* (bah-bah-LAHOS), practicing in Cuba. Santería attracts black, mulatto, and even white followers.

Roman Catholicism is still the dominant religion among white Cubans, and interest has grown steadily over the last thirty years. In 1998, Pope John Paul II visited Cuba and was well-received by President Fidel Castro. But the Catholic Church has still not won over many black and mixed-race Cubans, who find the informality of Santería very appealing. Of the 260 Catholic priests in Cuba, only two are black.

In the 1960s, the Cuban government criticized organized religion as being counterrevolutionary and forced many Catholic, Protestant, and Jewish clergy members to leave the country. Thus, many Cubans became nonreligious or atheist, and churchgoers were frowned upon. Today, almost half the Cuban population is nonreligious, but organized religion is making a comeback.

Below: **A Santerían fiesta parades through a Havana street. Since Santerían priests, or babalawos, practice from their homes, Santería (unlike Catholicism, Judaism, and Protestantism) was not very affected by the religious restrictions imposed by the Cuban government during the 1960s.**

Language and Literature

The Spanish Influence

All Cubans speak Spanish, but some expressions from the West African Yoruban language are also used. Spanish was introduced to Cuba by explorers and conquistadors and quickly became the national language. Yoruban, introduced by African slaves, was preserved in Santerían religious culture. Unfortunately, native Cuban Indian languages never survived the domination of the Spanish empire.

Spanish and English have the same alphabet. Spanish phonetics, however, contain two sounds that are not found in English: the "rr," which is produced by flapping the tongue, and the "j," which sounds like a hard English "h." Still, many English speakers find Spanish a simple language to learn because of the similar vocabularies. For example, most words ending in "–tion" in English are virtually the same in Spanish, only ending in "–ción," such as *conversación* (cohn-vehr-sah-SYONE).

Left: **An outdoor Havana bookstall carries several books either by or about revolutionary hero Che Guevara.**

Powerful Pens

Some of Cuba's greatest writers — José Martí, Nicolás Guillén, and Che Guevara — also happen to be Cuba's greatest social activists and revolutionary heroes. Martí was famous for his expressive poetry and essays that reflected his passionate desire to liberate Cuba from Spain in the late 1800s. Guillén, Cuba's most celebrated poet and equal rights activist, often explored his African heritage in his writing, incorporating Afro-Cuban musical rhythms into his poetry. Che Guevara's writings include political commentaries, a manual on guerrilla warfare, and candid memoirs from his combat days in the 1959 revolutionary war.

Cuba's greatest novelist, Alejo Carpentier, was also a journalist, diplomat, and musicologist. His novel, *The Lost Steps*, tells of a composer who travels deep into the jungle in search of the origins of music. Many Cuban writers share a common approach of blending refined literary style with popular slang expressions and "street talk." The results are well-appreciated by both laymen and intellectuals.

Above: **Potential customers browse through newspapers at a roadside newsstand in Guantánamo.**

Arts

Cuban arts are a blend of many different cultures, with African and Spanish influences being the strongest. The Cuban government fully supports local artists at both the student and professional level. The National Cultural Council, founded in 1961, is committed to recovering and dignifying Cuban cultural traditions and ensuring that working artists can make a living.

Music

Afro-Cuban music is one of the most influential in the world — its sounds and rhythms are often incorporated into rock 'n' roll, pop, rhythm and blues, funk, and jazz music. Salsa is a popular style of dance music that has strong Afro-Cuban, Caribbean, and jazz roots. The rhythmic element of salsa originates from Cuba's equivalent of the blues, called *son* (SONE). Salsa clubs can now be found in Europe, North America, and Japan.

Cuban jazz musicians, including pianist Gonzalo Rubalcaba and the group Irakere, are world famous. In the late 1940s, jazz

SALSA

With its pulsing rhythms and unique harmonies, salsa is one of the most exciting music styles in the world. Salsa has inspired countless musicians, composers, artists, choreographers, writers, and filmmakers.
(A Closer Look, page 66)

Below: A trio of guitarists enjoys an outdoor jam session. In Cuba, the street is one of the best classrooms for music instruction.

Above: **A modern dance troupe rehearses for a performance.**

great Dizzy Gillespie fused Afro-Cuban rhythms and bebop jazz to create Cubop. Today's Latin jazz descends directly from Cubop.

Favorite traditional Cuban musical forms include *Nueva Trova* (new-AY-vah TROH-vah) and *Punto Guajiro* (POON-toh gwa-HEE-roh). The sophisticated Nueva Trova, or "New Minstrels," merges poetry with traditional folk songs. Punto Guajiro, or Cuban country music, is often performed by roving street musicians who impress passersby with witty lyrics and flashy guitar playing.

Classical music is also popular among Cubans; even small cities have their own state-sponsored symphony orchestras.

Dance

Cubans consider dancing an essential part of experiencing their music. At outdoor music festivals, which are held throughout the year, people of all ages dance freely to complex salsa rhythms or Afro-Cuban jazz grooves.

The classical dance scene is dominated by the prestigious National Ballet of Cuba, founded in 1948 by dancer Alicia Alonso. The Modern Dance Company in Havana and the National Folk Company (a folk dancing troupe) are also very popular.

Visual Arts

Cuba's most famous visual artist was the painter Wilfredo Lam, who, like many great artists, chose to live in Paris. An exciting new movement among Cuban painters is "naive art." Most naive artists have no formal training in drawing or painting; their brilliantly colorful work depicts everyday urban and rural scenes.

Sculpture is another popular medium for Cuban artists. Styles range from revolutionary art to protest art, from Modernist forms to traditional themes. Santerían orishas are recurring images among more traditional artists. Cuban artisans work with wood, marble, ceramics, metal, hides, and also local materials, such as coconut fibers and snail shells.

The Ministry of Culture promotes Cuban art by providing artists with schools (such as the Higher Institute of Art), raw materials, and job placement services (usually in the design industry). In 1984, the government founded a semiannual international festival called the Havana Biennial, which showcases art from Third World countries. Cuba's main avenues for art exhibition are the National Museum of Fine Arts, the Gallery of Havana, and the Haydée Santamaría Gallery.

Above: **A Cuban artist paints landscapes in his Santiago studio. In Cuba, artists are regarded as professionals; this scenario differs from other countries, where many artists are forced to work at other jobs and practice their art on the side.**

Architecture

A number of sixteenth-century structures have survived in older Cuban cities such as Havana, Santiago, Trinidad, and Remedios. The Spanish colonial, or baroque, style of the 1700s features intricate stonework, detailed black-iron balconies, sculpted pillars, and elaborate window frames. In the 1800s, Cuban architects adopted simpler neoclassical styles. Today, Cuban architects are busy restoring old architectural relics as well as inventing more modern styles.

Film

Since the early 1960s, Cuba has been a dynamic scene for film directors, screenwriters, and actors. Aspiring filmmakers from all over the world study cinema at the Cuban Institute of Cinematographic Art and Industry. Cuba's most acclaimed director was Tomás Gutiérrez Alea (1928–1996), whose films often combined humor, romance, and social satire. His last film, *Guantanamera* (gwahn-tah-nah-MEH-rah), was a political satire that won international praise.

OLD HAVANA

Cuba's oldest and most magnificent buildings are found in Old Havana, a small precinct within the capital that dates back to the early 1500s. A well-preserved city of the past, Old Havana continues to fascinate visiting historians, architects, urban planners, and tourists from around the world.
(A Closer Look, page 58)

Left: **One of the most lavishly decorated buildings in Cuba, the National Theater (also called the García Lorca Theater, after the Spanish poet Federico García Lorca) stands on the Prado, an avenue that runs along the outskirts of Old Havana.**

Leisure and Festivals

Social interaction in Cuba is intense. Formal neighborhood organizations and informal gatherings bring people together constantly. Family activities often spread casually down the hall and even down the block. For example, when a popular television program is going to be aired, residents with a television set call out to their neighbors to come and watch. On weekends, families leave their front doors open, and people walk in and out freely. Privacy is not a Cuban cultural priority.

Public parks, street corners, and coffee counters attract regular crowds of people who, day and night, discuss the neighborhood news, political events, and personal stories. Not surprisingly, a favorite Cuban gathering place is the beach, where people can relax, cool off, and meet with friends. In Havana, when people are too busy to venture out to the beach, they retreat to the *Malecón* (mah-leh-CONE), a wall that traces the seaward edge of the city. The Malecón is an after-school, after-work, fishing, cycling, and shopping hangout all rolled into one.

THE MALECÓN

The Malecón is a stone wall that protects the north side of Havana from the pounding waves of the sea. Every day, thousands of Cubans and tourists flock to the Malecón to relax, chat with friends, hang out, and stroll by the seaside.
(A Closer Look, page 54)

Below: A Havana bar keeps both Cubans and foreign tourists entertained. Tourists appreciate the relaxed openness of Cuban social life.

Games

Cubans play a variety of games to occupy leisure time. Dominoes and chess are especially popular among teenagers and adults; senior citizens often play dominoes in cafés and city parks. Children prefer marbles and *bolero* (bo-LEH-roh), a game that involves a wooden cup and a ball that is connected to the cup by a long string. To play the game, a player holds the cup, swings the ball into the air, and attempts to catch it perfectly in the cup.

Cycling

Cycling has always been popular in Cuba, but after the 1991 Soviet breakup, oil shortages made bicycles a necessity. Fidel Castro proclaimed "the era of the bicycle," and the government gave free bicycles to all Cubans who did not already own one. People were encouraged to cycle to work and use pedal-power for all local traveling needs. Cycling along the beach is a favorite Cuban activity. In Havana, a special bus, called a *cyclobus* (see-cloh-BOOSE), has a bike ramp that allows cyclists to board the bus with their bicycles and be taxied to more distant parts of the city.

Above: **A competitive chess match attracts some local attention in Cardenas. No activity in Cuba remains a solitary affair.**

Sports

In 1961, the Cuban government created the National Institute of Sports to promote sports activities throughout the country. Professional sports were abolished, and, suddenly, all Cubans enjoyed free access to athletic facilities and inexpensive tickets for spectator sports. Today, sports such as basketball, volleyball, softball, and baseball are extremely popular among Cuban youths — not just as exercise, but as fun social gatherings.

Baseball is Cuba's most played and watched sport. Some of Cuba's greatest baseball players are now playing in major league baseball in North America. Cuba sponsors national tournaments in boxing, cross-country cycling, weight lifting, track and field, fencing, and chess. The government's serious commitment to physical education has paid off quickly. Over the last thirty years, Cuban athletes, both men and women, have won Olympic medals in boxing, track and field, volleyball, swimming, and baseball. Since the mid-1970s, Cuba has led all other Latin American countries in both the Pan-American Games and the Summer Olympic Games.

Above: **Schoolchildren compete in a basketball drill during physical education class. Basketball is a popular playground sport.**

BASEBALL

When it comes to sports, baseball is Cuba's national pastime. Cuba and the United States have a long history as baseball competitors, and the rivalry continues as major league baseball attracts more and more Cuban players.

(A Closer Look, page 44)

Teófilo Stevenson

Teófilo Stevenson is an international boxing legend and a hero to most Cubans. After winning a gold medal in the 1972 Olympic Games, Stevenson was approached by boxing promoters to fight U.S. boxer Muhammad Ali for the world heavyweight championship. Stevenson refused, however, since he was more interested in his studies and the socialist revolution than making money. In the 1976 Olympic Games, Stevenson knocked out his first three opponents in a record 7 minutes and 22 seconds on his way to a second gold medal. Finally, at the 1980 Olympic Games held in Moscow, Stevenson became the first boxer to win three Olympic gold medals in the same division (heavyweight).

The Cuban government has praised Stevenson's dignity, unselfishness, and athletic prowess. Today, Stevenson is regarded as both a world-class athlete and a revolutionary role model. In the 1990s, U.S. agents have offered multimillion dollar contracts to many Cuban athletes to play professionally in the United States. Following Stevenson's example, many Cubans have chosen to reject these offers and remain in Cuba to play for their country and to please their hometown fans.

Below: **Olympic champion Teófilo Stevenson** *(center)* **makes many public appearances at national sporting events, such as the Havana Marathon, to encourage fellow athletes and fans.**

Festivals

Latin American festivals, whether wild or restrained, are usually connected with Catholic traditions. Cuba, however, remains the most secular of all Latin American countries, and, thus, most Cuban festivals are secular, or nonreligious. A number of Cuban festivals are also specific to a certain city or region.

Carnaval, Cuba's oldest and most important festival, is a traditional celebration that dates back to 1493, when Christopher Columbus first introduced sugarcane to Cuba. During the Spanish colonial era, the end of the sugarcane harvest sparked a joyous festival among the African slaves who toiled in the fields. Today, most Cubans celebrate Carnaval from late July to early August; a pre-Lenten version of Carnaval takes place in Havana in February. Parading dancers march through the streets, parties spread contagiously, and the music never stops playing.

Havana opens its doors to a variety of international cultural festivals. The biannual Havana International Jazz Festival, held in December, invites star-caliber jazz players to dazzle a city of jazz lovers and to rediscover Afro-Cuban musical roots. Other biannual festivals in Havana include the International Guitar

CARNAVAL

Carnaval is Cuba's most widely celebrated festival. Since Carnaval coincides with the anniversary of Fidel Castro's rebellion against Fulgencio Batista, the weeks of parading and partying take on a patriotic meaning as well.
(A Closer Look, page 46)

Below: Dancers always play a big part in Cuban celebrations such as Carnaval, Las Parrandas, and various music festivals.

Left: **Cuban festivals reflect multicultural influences. These young Santerían paraders celebrate their African, Cuban, and Spanish heritage.**

Festival (May), the International Theater Festival (summer), and the International Festival of Latin American Film (December).

The Romería de Mayo (the May Pilgrimage) is a religious festival that takes place in the city of Holguín, in eastern Cuba. Pilgrims arrive during the first week in May, ascend Loma de la Cruz (Hill of the Cross), and visit the cross placed there by the Spaniards in the late 1700s to ward off drought. Holguín also hosts the Ibero-American Culture Festival in October and the biannual International Ballet Festival in November.

Since the 1800s, Christmastime in the colonial town of Remedios has always been celebrated as Las Parrandas (the Wild Days), an entertaining competition between neighborhoods to see which one can produce the best, most elaborate, most memorable parade floats, called *carrozas* (cah-RROH-sahs). Celebrated on the last Saturday of the year, Las Parrandas festivities include street fairs, music, dancing, and fireworks.

Food

When Fidel Castro declared Cuba's "special period" in 1991, the national diet was one of the first things to be affected. Before 1991, many Cubans survived on a high-calorie, high-fat, high-cholesterol, low-fiber diet made up of imported foods. After the withdrawal of Soviet aid, Cuban agriculture (based almost entirely on sugarcane) suddenly had to provide the national food supply.

In the 1990s, the government tried to replace imported rice and wheat in the Cuban diet with sweet potatoes and *yuca* (YOO-cah) — two starchy vegetables that could be grown domestically. Organic agriculture put more fruits and vegetables on the Cuban dinner table, and pig farms provided a staple meat product: pork. *Lechón* (leh-CHONE), or roast pig prepared with bitter orange and garlic, is one of Cuba's prized delicacies. A popular vegetarian dish is *congris* (cohn-GREESE), or rice with black beans; it is often served with a salad, yuca with garlic,

SNACKS AND SWEETS

Cuba has a quality menu of snacks, drinks, sweets, and finger food. Casual food vendors play a delicious role in everyday Cuban life.
(*A Closer Look*, page 68)

Below: A Cuban shops for pork at a Chinese butcher's stall. Pork is common in the Cuban diet because it is very affordable.

Above: **An El Rápido waitress on roller skates serves up a tray of fast food to a hungry family.**

fried banana, and fruit to make a nutritious and tasty meal. Cuban tastes tend to be milder than the spicy cuisines of Latin American countries.

Food Rations

Cubans obtain subsidized food products through a monthly rationing system, in which everyone is entitled to the same quantities of basic food necessities at reduced prices. During times of scarcity, children, senior citizens, and the seriously ill receive more rations than other citizens. Food rations do not last the entire month, however, so most Cubans tend a vegetable garden, barter for food, or buy additional food.

Restaurants

Private restaurants, once outlawed in Cuba, were legalized in the mid-1990s, although they are restricted to four tables or less. These *paladares* (pah-lah-DAR-ehs) are often found in apartment dining rooms and serve authentic, home-cooked food. Few fast-food restaurants exist in Cuba, since U.S. companies are prohibited (by U.S. law) from trading with Cuba. A government fast-food chain called El Rápido offers hot dogs and hamburgers.

WHEELS OF AGE

The U.S. trade embargo and the Soviet collapse have turned Cuba into a history museum of transportation. Vintage cars and steam-engine locomotives roam (and often sputter) throughout the country, aged but well-preserved by the most resourceful mechanics in the world.

(A Closer Look, page 70)

A CLOSER LOOK AT CUBA

Within Hispanic America, or the Spanish-speaking countries of the Americas, people share many common cultural characteristics, including language, social customs, colonial history, and family values. Despite these general similarities, each Hispanic-American nation has a unique identity in terms of ethnic makeup, class structure, politics, religious customs, art, and daily lifestyle. These distinctions are magnified in the case of Cuba, which, for the last forty years, has remained in relative isolation from the United States and has embarked on controversial social experiments totally foreign to its neighboring nations.

Opposite: A teacher instructs a young girl in a primary school reading class. In Cuba, women have achieved equal representation in professional fields such as teaching, banking, and medicine.

This section examines, in greater detail, some of the more fascinating aspects of the Cuban experience — from well-known Cuban icons (cigars, Che Guevara, baseball, and salsa music) to the little-known cultural delights (the Malecón, old-fashioned neighborhood charm, vintage automobiles, and Cuban ice cream). The landmark achievements of the Cuban government also merit a closer look, especially the elimination of racial and gender discrimination and the development of a sustainable, chemical-free, organic agriculture system.

Above: Shoppers, vendors, cyclists, and tourists gather in the central square of Sancti Spiritus, a city in southern central Cuba. Open plazas and town squares are an essential part of community interaction.

Baseball

Baseball is Cuba's national sport. The Cuban baseball league is one of the best in the world, and the national team has the Olympic gold medals to prove it. Baseball also plays a major part in Cuba's recreational culture. Most Cuban neighborhoods have their own baseball teams, and stickball is a celebrated tradition in the streets of Havana. Softball is played by both males and females, and women's teams often compete against men's teams.

The Cuban baseball season begins in November, just after the World Series, which closes the major league baseball season in North America. Before the 1959 revolution, this schedule let many major league baseball players stay in shape by playing "winter ball" in warm and sunny Cuba. After Castro took power, however, Cuban authorities decided to develop a more independent baseball league that excelled without foreign influences. Baseball, like the economy, became nationalized.

PROUD PLAYERS

During the 1996 Olympic Games in Atlanta, Omar Linares, a star infielder for the Cuban baseball team, was courted by several major-league baseball teams. Amidst all the rumors of his possible defection, he remarked, "I'd rather play for 11 million Cubans than 11 million dollars."

Left: A young Cuban stickball player awaits his turn at the plate. Like New York City, Havana is a baseball town, where people can enjoy the game anywhere — in stadiums, parks, schoolyards, or even back-alley streets.

Cuban baseball players were asked to remain in the Cuban league in order to foster a competitive wave of players and coaches. By the 1980s, Cuba's national baseball team dominated international competitions, often against all-star teams of future major leaguers. But Cuban baseball stars led very different lives from major league baseball stars, whose salaries were skyrocketing into millions of dollars. In socialist Cuba, even a baseball star was expected to live like the rest of the population and hold down a job (usually as a physical education teacher). Scouting agents often lured Cuban baseball players to defect to the United States and play major league baseball. Surprisingly, a number of Cuba's top players rejected lucrative major league contract offers, choosing instead to remain in Cuba to please their loyal fans.

During the 1990s, as the national economy struggled, Cuban players were allowed to play in foreign baseball leagues on the condition that they contributed half their salaries to the Cuban government. In the spring of 1999, the Cuban national team and the Baltimore Orioles, a major-league ball club, squared off in a historic, two-game series. In Havana, the visiting Orioles defeated the Cubans, 3–2; in Baltimore, Maryland, the Cubans won, 12–6.

Above: **Starting pitcher Liván Hernández helped the Florida Marlins win the 1997 World Series. A former star in the Cuban baseball league, Hernández defected to the United States and is now one of the best pitchers in the National League. Liván's half-brother, Orlando "El Duque" Hernández, pitches for the New York Yankees and helped lead them to a World Series title in 1998.**

Carnaval

Carnaval is the biggest annual celebration in Cuba. The secular version of Carnaval, which celebrates the end of the midsummer harvest, starts in July and is centered around the city of Santiago de Cuba. Havana's Carnaval, held in February, follows the Roman Catholic tradition of celebrating the last days leading up to Lent, a period of fasting and penitence before Easter.

Cuba's secular Carnaval is a cultural remnant of the early Spanish empire. Colonial plantation owners had traditionally given their slaves a post-harvest, week-long rest period that later evolved into Carnaval. Since most of these slaves were Yorubans, Carnaval festivities include many West African customs, such as singing and dancing in praise of orishas. The celebration is a lively, outdoor affair, as musicians and *comparsas* (kom-PAR-sahs), or dancing troupes, perform in the streets, donning elaborate, colonial-era costumes in a fun attempt to turn back the clock.

The Cuban government canceled Carnaval from 1991 through 1996 because of the nation's economic troubles. Fortunately, Cuban trade and commerce recovered well enough for Carnaval festivities to be renewed in 1997.

Below: **Musicians, dancers, and spectators crowd the Havana streets during Carnaval. Although Havana's Carnaval, like Mardi Gras in New Orleans, is associated with the Christian season of Lent, non-Christians often take part in the fun and festivities.**

Left: **A young Cuban woman shows off her colorful clothes. Carnaval is not just a vacation, but a meaningful celebration of cultural heritage.**

Anniversary of the National Rebellion

Santiago's Carnaval coincides with the anniversary of Fidel Castro's daring attack on the Moncada military base on July 26, 1953. This attack landed Castro in prison, but it strengthened his will for revolution. Castro later founded the 26th of July Movement, which eventually triumphed over Batista in 1959. Every year, on July 26, Cubans celebrate their most important public holiday, the Anniversary of the National Rebellion, featuring marching parades, street parties, and public speeches by Fidel and Raúl Castro. Many patriotic Cubans wave flags or wear armbands marked "M•26•7," indicating the birthday of the Movement.

Cigars

Tobacco has always been a major part of Cuban culture. By the time Christopher Columbus landed in Cuba in 1492, the native Cuban Indians had been smoking crudely fashioned tobacco cigars for hundreds of years. The word *cigar* actually comes from a South American Indian language.

The Spaniards initially had mixed feelings about tobacco. In the early days of the Spanish empire, the colonial church banned tobacco, before realizing a better solution — taxing it. In 1717, the first Cuban rebellion against Spanish rule happened because the rebels opposed the tobacco tax on cigars.

How a Leaf Becomes a Cigar

Cuba has almost 500 years of experience as a commercial tobacco producer. The island's coastal plains, especially in the province of Pinar del Río, are well-suited for growing tobacco. The best tobacco is grown on small farms where each plant receives personal care.

Left: **A tobacco farmer collects dried tobacco leaves. The leaves are fermented before they are rolled into cigars.**

Tobacco is grown during the dry season, when the days are warm, the nights are cool, and there is a minimum of rainfall. Farmers plant seedlings in November and harvest the crop in March. The leaves are then sorted and left to dry for about a month. After drying, the leaves are fermented, which mellows the flavor of the tobacco and lowers the tar and nicotine content. Most good cigars are double-fermented.

A smaller section of the tobacco crop grows under a canopy of cheesecloth, which blocks the wind and excess sunlight. These specially pampered leaves will become the *capa* (KAH-pah), or wrapper, of the finest cigars.

Factory workers roll the fermented tobacco leaves into cigars by hand. Each cigar is made from cut tobacco that is packed within a binder leaf; the *capa* is wound spirally around the filled binder leaf to make a neat package. Traditionally, cigar factory workers were entertained by a *lector* (lek-TORE), who reads the daily newspaper and other literature during the hours of rolling.

Cigars come in a variety of shapes and sizes. Cubans prefer the long, round-ended corona or the short and stout robusto; these thick-shaped cigars burn longer and cooler than smaller, thinner cigars. Cigarettes are made from the tobacco leaves rejected by cigar factories.

Above: Workers patiently cut and roll tobacco leaves in a typical Cuban cigar factory. Although it looks easy, rolling cigars is a skill that takes years to master.

Below: A Cuban happily poses with the finished product: a flavorful, carefully hand-rolled cigar.

Community

Foreigners are often astonished by the profound sense of community among Cubans. Friends and neighbors go out of their way to help people — not out of politeness, but out of honest sincerity. Social relationships between Cubans tend to be long-lasting, open, inclusive, and refreshingly relaxed.

Health experts believe that this sense of community contributes to the long life expectancy of Cubans by providing people with an emotional support system. Cuba may one day become a part of the "global village," but the local neighborhood will always remain the nucleus of Cuban social life.

Close-Knit Neighborhoods

Cuba is best described as a country of neighborhoods. All social, cultural, political, and economic activity revolves around intimate, self-contained neighborhood districts. Everyone matters in each of these tightly woven communities. Shopkeepers, cobblers, street musicians, street artists, and even black marketeers are all important to the neighborhood identity.

Below: Primary school students take a break from classes. Cuba's unique sense of community extends to all age groups.

Above: **A cobbler and a customer discuss the details of a job. Small shops foster very casual and friendly relations between the business operators and their customers.**

The health care system in Cuba is based on a network of neighborhood family doctors who must live on the same street on which they work (often in the same building of the medical clinic). Since every Cuban has a doctor as a neighbor, the system is remarkably efficient. People who have not had a medical checkup for more than half a year can expect a knock on the door from the neighborhood physician.

The main drawback of the neighborhood lifestyle is loss of privacy. In a community where everyone knows what everyone else is doing, solitude seems impossible. Outsiders may find Cuba's unrelenting social interaction suffocating, but, for Cubans, nosiness, gossip, and overly personal conversations are how they survive every day. A famous Spanish phrase is "small town, big hell." But in such a helpful and friendly small town, Cubans seem to be able to tolerate the accompanying "big hell."

Cubans who migrate to other countries often miss the neighborhood spirit of their homeland. Hopefully, these expatriates can teach their new neighbors the value of community culture.

Che Guevara

The story behind Fidel Castro's 1959 revolution is not complete without a closer look at Ernesto "Che" Guevara, whose famous image has become an icon for revolutionaries around the world. In Cuba, El Che's face is everywhere — on public buildings, classroom walls, billboards, murals, and storefront windows — while his spirit lives on in the hearts of most Cubans.

Guevara grew up in Argentina. As a teenager, he went on a motorcycle journey through Latin America, an experience that helped shape his lifelong political ambition of liberating the masses. In 1953, Guevara finished his studies to become a doctor and then traveled to Guatemala, where he witnessed the U.S.-supported military overthrow of a democratically elected, leftist government. This violent event triggered a revolutionary commitment in Guevara; his next move was to join Fidel and Raúl Castro in Mexico as they planned the 26th of July Movement that would overthrow Fulgencio Batista's regime in Cuba.

Below: **A roadside billboard depicts Che Guevara, one of the founding fathers of modern Cuba.**

CABALLERO SIN TACHA Y SIN MIEDO

During the guerrilla war that lasted from 1957 to 1959, Guevara served as a soldier and doctor for Castro's army. Despite asthma attacks that left him in frail health, Guevara fought so bravely that Castro put him in charge of a brigade. Guevara's troops won a decisive battle against Batista's soldiers in Santa Clara before marching on to Havana on January 2, 1959. A war hero, Guevara was appointed President of the National Bank of Cuba and Minister of Industry in the new government.

The Cuba-Soviet alliance soured Guevara's taste for politics. Cuban trade still relied on the export of sugar (only now, the buyer was the Soviet Union, not the United States), and the Soviets were not interested in modernizing the Cuban economy. Disenchanted, Guevara left his government post in 1965 to fight revolutions in other countries. After a brief assignment in the Congo, Guevara went to Bolivia, where he planned to stir up a mass revolt. The Bolivian civilians, however, did not unite behind him as the Cubans had in 1959, and the operation failed. The Bolivian army captured and executed Che Guevara in 1967.

In 1997, Guevara's remains were discovered in Bolivia and returned to Cuba for an official ceremony. Today, El Che is still revered for his bravery, passion, and commitment to his ideals.

Above: Two schoolboys stand in front of a wall mural bearing Che Guevara's famous face. Che Guevara remains a popular symbol of revolutionary ideals — not just in Cuba, but all over the world.

The Malecón

The Malecón is a stone seawall that stretches across Havana's north side, from the Old Havana district near the harbor entry to the upscale Vedado neighborhood near the Almendares River. A sidewalk runs parallel to the wall, and the quaint Malecón Avenue runs a few steps further inland. On the seaward side of the Malecón lie wave-battered rocks and the Gulf of Mexico.

The Malecón is one of Havana's greatest hangouts, an outdoor living room for people of all ages. In the mornings, casual fishermen arrive by bicycle and spread out along the wall, hoping to catch the evening's dinner. Kids rush to the Malecón when school finishes in the afternoon; a few fearless ones dive off an overhanging ledge into the ocean despite the huge rocks on the shore at the foot of the seawall. During the hot Havana summer, the Malecón is a favorite night spot, where families, friends, and couples can stroll along the boulevard and enjoy the cool sea breeze. The wall is also the best vantage point from which to view the beautiful Havana skyline. As the eye moves east to west, the

Below: **An experienced fisherman pulls in his line as two young boys eye his catch. The Malecón attracts all kinds of people and, occasionally, a big fish.**

cityscape transforms from fragile baroque structures to sturdy modern highrises. With all its local and tourist traffic, the Malecón is one of the most multicultural places in Cuba.

The most popular spot on the Malecón is called La Punta (The Point) where the land juts out to form a spacious gathering spot. La Punta offers a close view of *El Morro* (ehl MOH-roh), the colonial fortress that stands across the bay and once defended Havana against pirate attacks. Made of stone and mortar, El Morro features a lighthouse with a beacon that can be seen more than 40 miles (64 km) out to sea. Across the boulevard from La Punta, people who visit the Malecón on bicycle can hop on a cyclobus bound for El Morro. The bus travels through a tunnel to the other side of Havana Bay, where cyclists can ride around the fortress grounds and get a fantastic view of the harbor.

Every year on October 28, school lets out early, and all of Havana's students make a pilgrimage to the Malecón, where they throw flowers out to sea in honor of Camilo Cienfuegos, a revolutionary hero and compatriot of Fidel Castro. Cienfuegos died tragically in a plane crash at sea on October 28, 1959.

Above: **Cubans relax near La Punta, a popular stretch along the Malecón. In the background, the imposing El Morro guards the entry to Havana Bay.**

Mogotes

The province of Pinar del Río, located 112 miles (180 km) west of Havana, is the heart of Cuba's tobacco region. Like the rest of Cuba's lowlands, Pinar del Río has plenty of flat, rolling fields that are well-suited for agriculture. The local landscape, however, has a very odd-looking characteristic — it is dotted with massive, haunting, flat-topped mountains of limestone, called mogotes.

A stunning example of natural beauty, the mogotes are one of the most unusual geographic formations in the world. While most mountains have sloping sides, mogotes have vertical sides that form 90-degree angles with the ground. Underneath each

mogote's dense carpet of green foliage is a huge limestone outcrop that used to be underwater. The mogotes were the first formations to emerge from the Atlantic Ocean when Cuba was formed during the Jurassic Age, over 140 million years ago.

Water erosion has made the mogotes even more spectacular from the inside. Near the small, pine-treed town of Viñales, the mogotes hide remarkable labyrinths of caves and tunnels carved out by underground rivers. The most famous cave in this area is called Cueva del Indio. Visitors can walk through part of the cave for 300 yards (274 m), and then ride in a boat for 350 yards (320 m) on an underground river, until reaching a waterfall at the end of

Above: **The strangely shaped mogotes tower over the tobacco fields of Viñales, a small town in western Cuba. Mogotes are the oldest known rock formations on the island.**

the cavern. Beneath another mogote, a cave has been converted into a discotheque called El Palenque. Most of these caves remain unexplored and are inhabited by mosquito-eating bats, which sleep by day and fly out at night.

With its steep flat sides, a single mogote provides a natural canvas for bold artistic visions. In 1972, Cuban artist Ovigildo González, assisted by a team of farm workers, painted a mural measuring 50 feet (15 m) high and 75 feet (23 m) long on the side of a mogote. The mural depicts the prehistory of the region and is dominated by colors of the Cuban flag — red, white, and blue.

Pinar del Río remains a popular nature retreat for Cuban city dwellers. Students, families, and church groups often gather at comfortable resorts or more rugged mogote "base camps" for

Below: Ovigildo González's famed mogote-mural dwarfs the modest home of a tobacco farmer in Viñales. The mural is almost as tall as a five-story building.

some outdoor leisure. Activities include nature walks, fishing, bird-watching, hiking, mountain climbing, and spelunking. A well-known mogote campground in Viñales is called Las Dos Hermanas (The Two Sisters).

The valley of the mogotes may look like paradise, but, for Cuban farmers, it is home. Beneath the beauty of Pinar del Río's scenery lies a productive land that yields the best tobacco in the world. In addition to tobacco, a number of unusual plants thrive in the area, including the medicinal *almácega* (ahl-MAH-cey-gah) tree and the *mimosas sensitivas* (mee-MOH-sahs sen-see-TEE-vahs), the leaves of which curl up timidly after being touched.

Old Havana

Old Havana, the oldest precinct within the capital, is a fascinating time capsule of Cuba's Spanish colonial history. Tourists walking the narrow streets of Old Havana are constantly amazed by what they see — hundreds of buildings, plazas, churches, fortresses, and mansions that were built between the sixteenth and nineteenth centuries. These structures are so historically important that the United Nations Educational, Scientific, and Cultural Organization (UNESCO) declared Old Havana a World Heritage Site in 1982. But Old Havana is much more than an architectural museum; it is a living, breathing, and bustling community that is still the center of Havana's commerce and nightlife.

Left: **Many of the residential buildings in Old Havana have been lived in for more than 400 years. Windows and doorways are usually outlined by ornate archways and breezy balconies.**

HAVANA'S OLD CITY LIMITS

The Old Havana precinct is just 3 square miles (7.8 square km) in area. Havana Bay borders the precinct to the north, east, and south; Mission Avenue and Monserrate Avenue form the western boundary. At the north end of Old Havana stands a monument to General Máximo Gómez, the revolutionary leader who fought for Cuban independence with José Martí and Antonio Maceo in the late 1800s.

Preserving a National Treasure

During the 1960s and 70s, Cuban socialism saved Old Havana from reckless urban development. As Fidel Castro's revolution persuaded farmers to remain in rural areas to support national agriculture, Havana avoided the mass rural migration that turned many beautiful Latin American cities into chaotic urban sprawls during the twentieth century.

Old Havana is still protected by the revolution's laws against property speculation; it is further protected by its bicycle-riding residents, who help prevent the damaging effects of pollution and acid rain. But still, many of Old Havana's buildings are crumbling from a combination of age, neglect, and violent hurricanes. Since Old Havana faces the harbor, many of its building facades have been badly corroded by sea salt over the years.

The Cuban government and UNESCO are now collaborating on a major restoration plan to preserve Old Havana's architecture. Despite Cuba's struggling economy, the project is steadily progressing with financial aid offered by various universities, corporations, and foreign governments. The joint effort is spearheaded by Havana's city historian, Eusebio Leal Spengler.

Above: **The Spanish colonial architecture of Old Havana is distinctly colorful, with its pastel blues, yellows, pinks, and ochres. Stained glass above windows and doors are another common feature.**

Organic Rescue

After the United States enacted trade sanctions against Cuba in 1960, Cuba depended on the Soviet Union for economic aid. Favorable trade agreements made it cheaper for Cuba to export sugar and import foods than to grow its own food crops. For thirty years, Cuba was the only Latin American country that had eliminated starvation, even though its farmers produced little of the food its citizens ate. In 1991, the Soviet Union disintegrated, and Cuba was suddenly on the brink of a hunger crisis. Imported food supplies were cut off, so Cuba now had to produce its own food. However, imported gasoline (used for farming machines) and imported chemical fertilizers and pesticides were also cut off, leaving farmers paralyzed. The Cuban people needed food, the government could not buy it, and the farmers could not grow it.

The Cuban government decided to try out a boldly experimental method of agriculture, one that used organic, not

Below: Farmers in western Cuba harvest tobacco at the end of the dry season. After sugar, tobacco is Cuba's most important cash crop. As organic agriculture methods continue to succeed, the Cuban government hopes to balance sugar and tobacco crops with food crops: grains, fruits, and vegetables.

Left: **A young woman sells fresh fruits and vegetables in Havana's central market. Although organic agriculture has eliminated the Cuban hunger crisis, the government still must import vast quantities of food products, especially rice, cooking oil, and livestock.**

chemical, means to successfully raise crops. Initiated in 1991, this experiment was a risky one — if it failed, the people would starve. President Fidel Castro was banking on Cuba's strong human resources. Making up only 2 percent of Latin America's population, Cuba represented 11 percent of Latin America's scientists. Castro promptly put the nation's fate into their hands.

Cuban agricultural scientists, monitored by a team of concerned U.S. scientists, proposed to convert Cuba's single-crop agriculture, which relied heavily on man-made fertilizers and pesticides, to a low-input, sustainable agriculture, which uses natural plants and microbes to nourish soil and kill pests. By mid-1993, as famine loomed, scientists worked desperately to develop specialized biofertilizers and biopesticides from earthworms, plant bacteria, ants, and animal manure.

By 1997, Cuba had overcome its major food shortages. Outdoor farmers' markets offered healthy foods like avocados, cucumbers, oranges, and bananas. Cuba has made history with the first ever nationwide conversion to organic agriculture.

Pirates

Beginning in the sixteenth century, the Caribbean Sea became a lucrative hunting ground for pirates. The New World territories of the Spanish empire — Mexico, California, Peru, and the West Indies — yielded immense riches and resources, including gold, silver, silk, wool, leather, sugar, coffee, tobacco, wine, indigo, and cacao. In a colonial economy, however, the profits (usually in the form of gold or silver) had to travel a great distance in order to reach the beneficiary, and between the New World's riches and Spain's royal treasury lay the Atlantic Ocean. Pirates attacked wherever the Spanish gold was most vulnerable: in Caribbean shipping ports or aboard imperial galleons in the open sea.

The coastal cities of Cuba were especially ripe targets for pirate attacks since nature had bestowed the island with excellent harbors. The Spanish colonial government built

THE SIEGE OF SANTIAGO

The worst series of pirate attacks in Cuba happened between 1538 and 1562 in the city of Santiago. Captain Jacques de Sores led the most infamous of these attacks by making a night landing with four ships in Santiago Bay. As the residents slept, Sores's crew kidnapped the wealthiest and most powerful people of the city and then demanded a ransom of 80,000 pesos in gold. Sores held Santiago for thirty days and got his ransom. Afterwards, many distressed Santiago residents decided to move inland to the city of Bayamo.

Left: Pirate raids on the open sea were daring encounters. The most successful pirates used surprise tactics to ambush an unsuspecting crew.

massive stone fortresses to protect its harbors. The most famous of these strongholds is El Morro, an impressive, 400-year-old work of stone masonry overlooking Havana Bay.

The Makings of a Pirate

Most pirates actually started out as French or English patriots. In order to challenge the Spanish empire's monopoly in New World commerce, England and France authorized their sailors to attack and loot ships bearing the Spanish flag. These sailors, called corsairs, routinely attacked and killed the crews of Spanish ships, then went ashore to raid cities and towns, looting and destroying them. The corsairs had agreed to forfeit much of their loot to the governments that employed them, but, after realizing how much money they were denied, many corsairs began to operate independently — as pirates.

Pirates continued to make raids on Cuba until the 1830s. Since the end of the pirating era, Cuba's battle-scarred fortresses have become popular tourist attractions. The fortress guarding Santiago Bay has since been converted into Cuba's Museum of Piracy.

Above: **El Morro guarded the city of Havana from pirates and other foreign attackers during the 1700s. Spanish colonists also built a wall around the city's perimeter as a second line of defense, although the wall no longer remains today. In 1762, British Admiral Sir George Pocock finally broke through Havana's strong fortifications and occupied the city for six months.**

Race Relations

Before the 1959 revolution, black Cubans were seriously underrepresented in well-paying jobs in banking, commerce, and science, and overrepresented in low-paying, labor-intensive jobs in construction and domestic services. Outside the workplace, the environment was also unfairly segregated. Upper-class social clubs in Havana excluded blacks and mulattoes systematically, and even public services, such as recreation centers, openly discriminated by race.

After the triumph of the revolution, Fidel Castro called for an end to racial discrimination. The Cuban government eliminated all the legal pillars that supported racism and pushed for racial integration in all parts of society, from neighborhood assemblies to corporate offices. Cuba's antidiscrimination reforms were based on bold, liberal policies such as free health-care, desegregation of all sports and academic facilities, and free and

Left: **Multiracial families are common in Cuba. Racial integration in Cuban society is now a reality, not just a government policy.**

equal education. One particularly effective reform measure was eliminating private schools, which had been mostly white.

Today, racial discrimination has disappeared from the workplace, and racial harmony is visually evident in everyday Cuban life. On the streets of Havana, groups of friends almost always include blacks, whites, and mulattoes, with no single race dominating the group. In hospitals and clinics, physician staffs have become fully racially integrated in proportion to the racial distribution of the population. Even the Afro-Cuban religion Santería has earned an integrated following that includes many white worshipers. Supporters of the socialist revolution point to Cuba's racially integrated society as one of the most important goals achieved by Castro's government.

Some racial prejudices still exist, however. A number of white Cubans resent the government's promotion of so many blacks to important positions, and, although interracial marriage is widely accepted, some Cuban parents still discourage their sons or daughters from marrying someone of another race. Prejudice remains a private feeling for these Cubans, since anyone who expresses prejudiced opinions in public faces serious consequences.

Above: **At a young age, Cubans learn that friendships have no racial boundaries.**

THE FUTURE

The recent legalization of U.S. dollars has created new concerns for preserving Cuba's racial equality. Most U.S. dollar income "earned" by Cubans comes in the form of donations by family members working and living abroad, and these expatriate Cubans tend to be white. Thus, black Cubans are at an economic disadvantage.

Salsa

Cuba produces every imaginable type of music, including rock, folk, country, classical, and salsa, a rhythmic dance music with complex harmonies. A hybrid of Afro-Cuban, Spanish, Caribbean, and Afro-American musical traditions, salsa is an accessible music that is easy to absorb and appreciate. Cubans listen and dance to salsa in restaurants and public clubs, at neighborhood parties, and at organized music festivals. Since salsa overlaps with jazz music, salsa bands are usually heard at jazz festivals as much as at Latin music festivals. New York City, Miami, Chicago, Los Angeles, and Toronto have some of the best salsa scenes outside of Cuba.

Son

The greatest influence on salsa is the traditional and rural son, which is now being revived by many musicians. The African origins of son can be heard in its complex rhythms, which mix several overlapping beats, and its "call and response" vocal arrangements, which have a chorus answering to the lead

Below: **A modern salsa band performs at a music festival. Salsa bands often feature several vocalists who harmonize and make lyrical conversation-like exchanges.**

singer's statements or "calls." Son musicians use many different instruments, including the *tres* (TREYSS), a three-stringed guitar; the *marímbola* (mah-RIM-bo-lah), a thumb piano with five metal keys; claves, a pair of wooden sticks clacked against each other; and the conga, a tall cylindrical drum. More conventional instruments, such as trumpets, guitars, bongos, and maracas, complete the son ensemble.

Rumba

The urban version of son is called *rumba* (ROOM-bah); son and rumba combine to form salsa. Rumba is a neighborhood musical tradition reminiscent of Mississippi Delta blues or Brazil's religious Candomblé. More vigorous than the relaxed son, rumba is a festive street music driven by sharp, percussive beats. Early rumba musicians used makeshift rhythm instruments, such as sticks struck against differently pitched wooden boxes or spoons tapped against glass bottles. The hip-swaying, sidestepping dance maneuvers of rumba became a favorite of ballroom dancers in the early 1900s.

Above: **The most important element of salsa is rhythm. The texture of the beat is just as essential as the song's melody.**

BANDS

Contemporary Cuban salsa groups include Los Van Van, Jesús Alemany's Cubanismo, the Afro-Cuban All-Stars, Bamboleo, and NG La Banda. One of the best Cuban rumba bands is Los Muñequitos de Matanzas. Rumba musicians are often called "carriers," since they are continuing a musical tradition that originated in the 1800s.

Snacks and Sweets

Cubans have a big craving for snacks and sweets. Food and drink vendors are everywhere in Cuba — street corners, beaches, parks, and plazas — and provide a convenient, reliable service for people who must eat on the run. Unlike the heavily processed, packaged, and preserved foods common in today's fast-food culture, Cuban snacks are freshly prepared, served without frills or gimmicks, and deliciously simple.

Mobile peanut vendors often find the hungry masses before the masses find them. Peanuts are always freshly roasted and sold in paper cones. Popcorn is another Cuban favorite, enjoyed at the Malecón, the city markets, or the baseball stadiums. To wash down salty snacks, many Cubans prefer fresh fruit punch, which is healthier and cheaper (at just 1 CUP, or U.S. $0.04) than canned, carbonated soft drinks. Fruit-drink stalls also usually sell tasty, homemade pizza. At curbside coffee shops, loyal customers bring their own cups (sometimes made from old beer cans) to get their daily dose of hot, potent Cuban coffee. Small kiosks and roving

Below: **Some of the best places to eat in Havana are the outdoor food markets, which offer a variety of snacks.**

food vendors make a charming substitute for the overly commercialized and impersonal restaurant culture common in many countries today.

A Taste for Ice Cream

Cuba's greatest specialty in the realm of snack food is ice cream. Cuban ice cream ranks with baseball, cigars, Old Havana, and salsa music as a bona fide national treasure. In fact, Cuban ice cream is much more than just a snack food or a dessert — it is often the focus of social occasions, such as family outings, casual get-togethers, and parties.

Above: **A young woman enjoys a fresh slice of cream cake from a Havana bakery.**

Cuba's most famous ice-cream brand is Coppelia, which has outlets all over the country. Havana's largest ice-cream parlor is Coppelia Ward, which seats eighty people (and employs up to forty on hot days when customers want their ice cream served up quickly). Ice cream comes in a variety of flavors, including the usual vanilla, strawberry, and chocolate, along with several tropical fruit flavors. At Coppelia Ward, a scoop of ice cream costs about 0.70 CUP, or less than U.S. $0.03.

Wheels of Age

Almost everything on wheels in Cuba is fortunate to still be running at all. Most vehicles on the road today were made before 1960, when the United States cut off most of its economic ties to Cuba. Subsidized Soviet gasoline powered these cars, trucks, and motorcycles until 1991, when the Soviet Union collapsed. Now faced with severe gasoline and mechanical parts shortages, only the most committed Cuban drivers can keep their aging, gas-guzzling wheels moving.

Automobiles and Buses

Visitors to Cuba gawk in amazement at the 1940s, 50s, and 60s cars cruising the streets. Vintage Fords, Chevrolets, and Plymouths with majestic tail fins and shiny chrome stripes lend a classic, old-fashioned feel to every Cuban city and town. Many of these cars would be worth a fortune in other countries, but, for Cubans, they are just another means of everyday, private

Below: **A parked, turquoise Chrysler embellishes a Havana street. With the U.S. trade embargo and the struggling national economy, Cubans must rely on old cars, buses, and motorcycles for transportation.**

transportation. Buses in Cuba are also outdated dinosaurs. A *camello* (cah-MEY-yoh), or "camel," is a crudely fashioned bus, made from a humped cabin trailer pulled by an old truck engine.

Above: **Patriotic bikers raise the Cuban flag over a vintage Harley Davidson motorcycle.**

Motorcycles

Sharing the road with classic cars, Cuba's fleet of mid-twentieth-century Harley Davidson motorcycles personifies not just finely crafted machinery but also a bold movement in automotive style. Motorcycle mechanics rely on scrappy, enthusiastic innovation to keep these machines in shape. Both desperation and gasoline fuel Cuban road warriors.

Trains

Cuba is the only Caribbean country that still has a railway system. The Cuban Central Railway, which crosses most of the island from Havana to Santiago, was built, between 1900 and 1902, by Sir William Van Horn, the founder of the Canadian Pacific Railway. Today, many nineteenth-century, U.S.-built steam locomotives are still chugging down these tracks, hauling both freight and passengers.

Women of the Revolution

Before the 1959 revolution, most Cuban women were restricted by the overwhelming sense of *machismo* (mah-CHEES-moh) in Latin American culture. "Machismo" is a Spanish word that refers to a cultural attitude in which male dominance of the household is accepted as the rule. Husbands expected their wives to do all the housework, raise the children, and cook for the family. Even working wives were expected to be obedient to their husbands and perform all of the household duties by themselves.

One of the major principles of the Cuban revolution was equality for women. In 1959, the revolutionaries initiated a nationwide effort, involving educators, filmmakers, and government officials, to convince the public that machismo was wrong and that women deserved the same chances in life as men.

Below: Cuban women enjoy equal opportunities at work, at home, and in their spare time.

Above: **Today, Cuban women make valuable contributions in the fields of science and medicine. This woman is a scientist in a biotechnology lab.**

Government programs, such as free child care, free health care, and food rationing, were specifically designed to free women from their traditional roles. With all Cubans guaranteed their basic needs, women who felt trapped in bad marriages could now divorce their husbands without worrying about the welfare of their children. To further encourage women to work, the government enforced equal employment practices that guaranteed equal salaries for men and women who had the same job position.

The results of these programs have been extremely liberating for Cuban women. Working women are now treated with as much dignity as working men. Today, there are as many female doctors in Cuba as male doctors. Business newspapers, an industry traditionally dominated by men, are now managed and edited by women. Female Cuban athletes have won Olympic gold medals in volleyball and track-and-field events, and, even in neighborhood sports such as softball, women's teams often compete against men's teams. In fact, Cuban women have become so successful academically and professionally that some of them feel guilty for not being able to fulfill a role in the home. Similarly, many housewives feel an enormous pressure to pursue a professional career, even if they are happy staying at home.

RELATIONS WITH NORTH AMERICA

Cuba has very opposite relations with the United States and Canada. After the 1959 revolution, U.S.-Cuban relations became hostile, culminating in the 1961 Bay of Pigs invasion and the 1962 Cuban missile crisis. The U.S. government is still strongly opposed to Fidel Castro and has maintained a tight economic embargo against Cuba since 1960. Upon severing all diplomatic, political, and economic ties to Cuba, U.S. government officials have repeatedly tried (with little success) to influence other foreign governments to do the same.

Below: **On a billboard in Havana, a gun-toting Cuban shouts to the growling Uncle Sam, "We're not scared of you Mr. Imperialist!" Anti-U.S. propaganda is a common sight in socialist Cuba.**

Canada, on the other hand, has stood by Cuba and supported the Castro regime's right to independent rule. In open defiance of the U.S. campaign to isolate Cuba from the international community, Canada continues to keep up trade and diplomatic relations with Cuba.

Despite the U.S.-Cuban standoff, Cuba's relaxed culture has made welcomed inroads into American life. Salsa, Cubop, Cuban athletics, and Little Havana all offer Americans an unforgettable taste of Cuban heritage.

Opposite: **Three high school students enjoy their ice cream cones while standing in front of a mural-size, anti-U.S. political cartoon. The cartoon shows Uncle Sam pouring poison into the television media.**

Controversy over the *Maine*

Cuba's first revolutionary war against the Spanish, also known as the Ten Years' War, lasted from 1868 to 1878 and ended in a stalemate. The revolution had lost its momentum, and the rebels had failed to attract a foreign ally. By the time war broke out again in 1895, however, the United States had investments in Cuba totalling fifty million dollars. Revolutionary General Máximo Gómez hoped that the United States would become the supporting player the rebels needed to win Cuban independence.

In January 1898, the United States sent a battleship, the USS *Maine*, to Havana Bay to protect U.S. citizens caught in the crossfire between Spanish and Cuban revolutionary forces. The unexplained sinking of the *Maine* by a violent explosion, on February 15, 1898, prompted a massive popular backlash against Spain in the United States. Although the cause of the explosion was never determined, the U.S. government declared war on Spain on April 25, 1898.

Historians have debated whether or not the United States used the sinking of the *Maine* as an opportunity to turn Cuba into a "neocolony," whose political and economic affairs would be controlled by the U.S. government. While the United States did help Cuba gain its independence from Spain in the resulting Spanish–American War of 1898, the Cuban rebels were rewarded with U.S. military occupation instead of freedom. Sadly, the U.S. intervention Gómez had desired backfired in the long run, since victory went to the U.S. government, not the Cuban people.

Opposite: **A political cartoon drawn in 1903 depicts the young, wealthy, and newly independent Cuba able to take care of itself, even though Uncle Sam looks very skeptical. Many people objected to U.S. neocolonialism in Latin America because it bolstered U.S. power while not necessarily promoting local democracy.**

Left: **This Havana monument remembers the sinking of the U.S. battleship, the *Maine*, on February 15, 1898. Sensationalized by U.S. newspapers, the event triggered U.S. intervention in Cuban affairs for the next sixty years.**

"I COME TO BUY, NOT TO BEG, SIR"

The Bay of Pigs Invasion

Fidel Castro's overthrow of Fulgencio Batista in 1959 was a turning point in U.S.-Cuban relations. In 1960, after the Cuban government expropriated U.S.-owned property and industries, the United States suspended all Cuban sugar purchases, cutting off 80 percent of Cuba's export trade. When the Soviet Union stepped in to buy Cuba's unwanted sugar, the U.S. government responded with an economic embargo that prohibited U.S. companies from trading with Cuba. Early in 1961, the United States broke off all diplomatic relations with Cuba.

Behind the scenes, the U.S. Central Intelligence Agency (C.I.A.) had sponsored a series of foiled assassination attempts on Fidel Castro and, as of May 1960, had been planning an invasion of Cuba by using an army of Cuban exiles. On April 17, 1961, the 1,500 armed and C.I.A.-trained Cuban exiles landed at the Bay of Pigs on the southern coast of Cuba. The invading forces expected the support of the Cuban people, but Cuban citizens fought alongside the national army to repel the attack. Within two days, Castro's army crushed the invaders, capturing over 1,100 men. Castro ransomed the survivors for $53 million worth of food and medical supplies. Humiliated, the administration of President John F. Kennedy was widely criticized for authorizing the invasion.

Above: U.S. president John F. Kennedy was in office during two of the most crucial events in the history of Cuban-American relations: the 1961 Bay of Pigs invasion and the 1962 Cuban missile crisis.

The Cuban Missile Crisis

Cuban-Soviet ties, first established in 1960, were both economic and military. Pleased with a new communist ally in the western hemisphere, Soviet premier Nikita Khrushchev agreed to ship conventional and nuclear arms to Cuba. In October 1962, the U.S. government discovered that the Soviet military had installed a number of medium- and long-range ballistic missiles on Cuban soil. Since these missiles were well within reach of the continental United States, the world was suddenly struck with the possibility of global nuclear war.

On October 22, 1962, President Kennedy ordered a naval blockade of Cuba and commanded U.S. forces to seize any Soviet weapons shipments bound for Cuba. After days of exchanging anxious messages, Kennedy and Khrushchev finally struck a bargain on October 28: the missiles would be returned to the Soviet Union if the United States pledged never to invade Cuba. The crisis ended in November 1962, as both sides stuck to the terms of the deal. Fidel Castro, whom Khrushchev never consulted during the crisis, criticized the Soviets for bowing under pressure.

Below: **On October 17, 1962, demonstrators sat in Trafalgar Square in London, England to protest the Cuban missile crisis. Fear of a global nuclear war prompted numerous peace demonstrations all over the world.**

79

Post-Soviet U.S.-Cuban Relations

The Cold War kept the U.S. embargo against Cuba in effect for almost thirty years after the Cuban missile crisis. When the Soviet Union broke up in 1991, the U.S. Congress actually stiffened trade restrictions against Cuba. The 1992 Cuban Democracy Act cut off food shipments to Cuba from foreign branches of U.S. corporations. In 1996, the Cuban military shot down two planes piloted by members of Hermanos al Rescate, a Cuban exile organization based in Miami, Florida. The Cuban government alleged that the planes were illegally flying in Cuban air space. In response, the U.S. Congress passed the controversial Helms-Burton Act, which allows U.S. companies formerly owning property confiscated by the Cuban government to sue any foreign company currently utilizing that property. The Helms-Burton Act also prevents the lifting of the U.S. trade embargo until the Castro regime has ended.

Above: Canadian prime minister Jean Chrétien has developed a close rapport with Cuban president Fidel Castro. Contradicting the hostile U.S. policy toward Cuba, the Canadian government uses its power to partner with, not isolate, the Republic of Cuba.

Cuba and Canada: Fellow U.S. Neighbors

Unlike the United States, Canada has maintained relatively friendly relations with Cuba since the 1959 revolution. The Canadian government has consistently refused, under U.S. pressure, to break off diplomatic relations with Cuba. In 1962, when the United States urged members of the Organization of American States (OAS) to impose economic sanctions against Cuba, only Mexico and Canada, the immediate neighbors of the United States, refused to let U.S. interests dictate their policy toward Cuba.

Canada and Cuba find common ground in having an imposing superpower neighbor, the United States. Within both Canada and Cuba, U.S. influences cast an intimidating shadow over national politics, economics, and culture. Thus, Canada and Cuba have developed a mutually beneficial relationship to ensure the survival of their individual ways of life.

Clashing Views on Cuban Trade

Since Castro declared Cuba's "special period" in 1991, the U.S. government has tightened economic sanctions against Cuba, hoping to inflict more hardship on Cuban citizens and eventually provoke them into overthrowing their government. In contrast, the Canadian government has chosen to alleviate these same hardships by encouraging Canadian businesses to engage in commerce with Cuba. While the U.S. government condemns these businesses for supporting a repressive regime, the Canadian government appreciates them for supporting an isolated country locked in an uphill battle against a world superpower.

As one of Cuba's largest trading partners today, Canada continues to oppose the U.S. embargo against Cuba, but strict U.S. laws aimed at foreign companies are discouraging international business ventures in Cuba. Canadian businesses operating in Cuba feel particularly threatened by the 1996 Helms-Burton Act, which makes them vulnerable targets in the U.S. courts. The Canadian government claims that any such legal action violates international law.

By strengthening economic ties with Cuba, Canadian officials can openly criticize the offenses of the Castro regime, such as human rights abuses, without endangering diplomatic ties. In 1998, Canadian Prime Minister Jean Chrétien visited Cuba to inaugurate the Canadian-financed José Martí International Airport in Havana. While Chrétien praised the benefits of Canadian-Cuban economic cooperation, he also urged Fidel Castro to release political prisoners.

Below: A Cuban shipping port operates near a petroleum plant. Cuban commerce and industry, suffocated by the U.S. embargo, have been supported by Russian, Spanish, Chinese, Dutch, and Canadian traders since 1960. Today, Canada is one of the largest importers of Cuban agricultural and manufactured goods. Canadian businesses are also collaborating with the Cuban government in joint business ventures.

Immigrating North

Cuban immigration to North America is largely the result of turbulent U.S.-Cuban relations following the 1959 revolution. The most common destination for Cuban immigrants has been the United States, especially the city of Miami. Major U.S. cities such as New York City, Chicago, and Los Angeles also have growing Cuban immigrant populations. In Canada, Cuban immigrants have made new homes in Toronto, Ottawa, and Montreal. In the late 1990s, the Canadian government invited newly released Cuban political prisoners to immigrate to Canada.

Cuban immigration is a sensitive issue in the United States. During the 1960s, the U.S. government automatically declared all Cuban immigrants eligible for residency. In the 1980s, Fidel Castro cleverly used these relaxed U.S. immigration laws to rid Cuba of convicted criminals, mentally ill patients, and dissenters who opposed the revolution. Castro thus strengthened his hold onto power by exiling his political opposition to the United States.

In the early 1990s, following a riot in Havana, Castro allowed Cuba's seafaring emigrants, the balseros, the right to navigate to Florida, where they were welcomed by U.S. immigration officials. Although some never made it through the shark-infested waters, the wave of balseros continued as the Soviet collapse shattered economic conditions at home. President Bill Clinton eventually withdrew the U.S. invitation to immigrating balseros, who were then picked up at sea and taken to Guantánamo Naval Base. Critics noted the harsh unfairness of this change in policy — the United States, through its trade embargo, indirectly caused the desperate flight of the balseros, who were then forced to remain in Cuba by the U.S. Navy.

Cuban-American Society

Cuban immigrants to the United States and Canada have been much more fortunate than their Latin American counterparts. The first generation of Cuban immigrants included mostly white, upper-class, well-educated professionals in the banking, construction, and shipping industries. Later waves of Cuban immigrants came from minority or working-class backgrounds and found work in American factories and service industries. Today, a new Cuban-American generation plays a wide role in American business, politics, education, and popular culture.

Above: A young Cuban has his preferred country "tattooed" on his arm. Despite tense U.S.-Cuban relations, many Cuban citizens hope, one day, to live in the United States.

EXCEPTION TO THE RULE

The U.S. government's pro-Cuban immigration stance is a far cry from its strict policy toward other Hispanic American immigrants. While Cuban refugees are generally well-received by the United States, millions of Mexicans and Central Americans (who would be turned away by U.S. immigration officials) risk their lives every year, attempting to sneak into U.S. territory.

Opposite: Young Cuban-Americans in Miami take part in a fiesta. Just 230 miles (370 km) from Havana, Miami has a thriving community of Cuban immigrants.

Cultural Connections

The political conflicts between Cuba and the United States have always overshadowed the strong cultural bonds between these two countries. Ironically, during Cuba's thirty-year alliance with the Soviet Union, the Soviets living in Cuba steered clear of the local culture, while, up north, U.S. citizens shared many Cuban cultural traditions, from baseball to Latin jazz.

Cuban culture has always been one of the most accessible cultures to North Americans. Salsa music is enormously popular in the United States and Canada. Cuban-American pop singer Gloria Estefan, who often mixes salsa rhythms into her music, ranks among the most famous Cubans in the world. Other Cuban-American musicians, such as band leader Mongo Santamaría and singer Celia Cruz, offer jazzier versions of salsa. American sports have also opened the door for cross-cultural exchange; Cuban boxers, baseball players, and track and field athletes have wowed American spectators for decades. Cuban baseball greats include Luis Tiant of the Boston Red Sox, Liván Hernández of the Florida Marlins, and Orlando Hernández of the New York Yankees.

Below, left: Gloria Estefan is one of the most popular singers in the world. In 1998, she performed with singers Mariah Carey, Shania Twain, Celine Dion, and Aretha Franklin in a concert appropriately titled "Divas Live."

Below, right: After his half-brother Liván defected to the United States in 1996, Orlando "El Duque" Hernández, a Cuban baseball legend, was banned from playing in Cuba. Orlando later followed Liván's footsteps to both a major league baseball team and a World Series championship.

Left: James Moody *(left),* Luciano "Chano" Pozo *(center),* and Dizzy Gillespie *(right)* performed together at Cornell University in Ithaca, New York in 1948. Jazz legend Gillespie had approached Pozo, a Cuban conga drummer, to develop a new style of jazz that combined American bebop with Pozo's Cuban and West African musical background. Chano spoke no English, but he still taught Gillespie the complex art of Afro-Cuban rhythms. The end result was the innovative music called Cubop.

Little Havana

The center of Cuban-American culture lies in Little Havana, an enclave of Cuban immigrants within Miami, where Cubans have established night clubs, restaurants, banks, and social circles that reflect their traditional way of life. The earliest residents of Little Havana always hoped to return to Cuba, and they anxiously awaited the fall of the Castro government. By the 1990s, however, this attitude had faded. Today, most Cuban-Americans look forward to a bright future living in America.

Cuban Exiles

Cuban exiles in America still actively protest the Castro regime. When the United States and Cuba sponsored cultural exchanges in the 1990s, Cuban exile leaders staged demonstrations against visiting Cuban musicians and threatened to ostracize Cuban-American musicians if they performed in Cuba. Although many Cuban immigrants support the hard-line Cuba policy of the United States, a growing number of Cuban-Americans want to see the U.S. embargo lifted to ease the suffering of Cuban citizens.

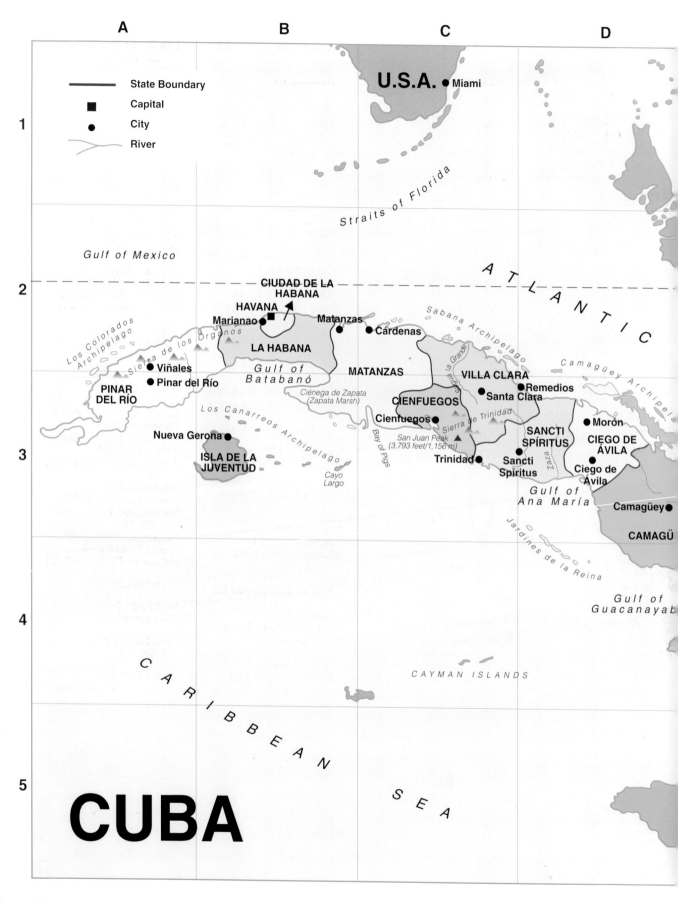

E   F

N

HE BAHAMAS

Tropic of Cancer

O C E A N

Nuevitas

LAS TUNAS
Las Tunas ● ● Holguín

HOLGUÍN ● Moa
Manzanillo Cauto
● ● Bayamo **SANTIAGO** **Baracoa**
GRANMA **DE CUBA** ●
Sierra Maestra Palma ● **GUANTÁNAMO**
Pico Turquino Soriano ● Guantánamo
(6,561 feet/2,000 m) ● Santiago ● Guantánamo
  de Cuba U.S. Naval Base

HAITI

JAMAICA

Atlantic Ocean C2–F3

Bahamas E1
Baracoa F4
Bay of Pigs C3
Bayamo E4

Camagüey (city) D3
Camagüey (province)
 D3–E3
Camagüey Archipelago
 D2–D3
Cárdenas C2
Caribbean Sea A4–D5
Cauto River E4
Cayman Islands C4
Cayo Largo B3
Ciego de Ávila (city) D3
Ciego de Ávila
 (province) D3
Ciénega de Zapata
 (Zapata Marsh) B3
Cienfuegos (city) C3
Cienfuegos (province)
 C3
Ciudad de la Habana B2

Granma E4
Guantánamo (city) F4
Guantánamo (province)
 F4
Guantánamo U.S. Naval
 Base F4
Gulf of Ana María D3
Gulf of Batabanó B2–B3
Gulf of Guacanayabo D4
Gulf of Mexico A2

Haiti F5
Havana B2
Holguín (city) E4
Holguín (province)
 E4–F4

Isla de la Juventud B3

Jamaica D5–E5
Jardines de la Reina
 D3–D4

La Habana B2
Las Tunas (city) E4

Las Tunas (province)
 E3–E4
Los Canarreos
 Archipelago B3
Los Colorados
 Archipelago A2

Manzanillo E4
Marianao B2
Matanzas (city) B2
Matanzas (province)
 B2–C2
Miami (U.S.) C1
Moa F4
Morón D3

Nueva Gerona B3
Nuevitas E3

Palma Soriano E4
Pico Turquino E4
Pinar del Rio (city) A3
Pinar del Rio (province)
 A3–B2

Remedios D3

Sabana Archipelago C2
Sagua la Grande River
 C2–C3
San Juan Peak C3
Sancti Spíritus (city) D3
Sancti Spíritus
 (province) C3–D3
Santa Clara C3
Santiago de Cuba (city)
 F4
Santiago de Cuba
 (province) E4–F4
Sierra de los Órganos
 A2–B2
Sierra de Trinidad C3
Sierra Maestra E4
Straits of Florida B2–C1

Trinidad C3

United States of
 America C1

Villa Clara C2–C3
Viñales A2

Zaza River D3

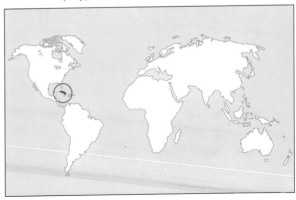

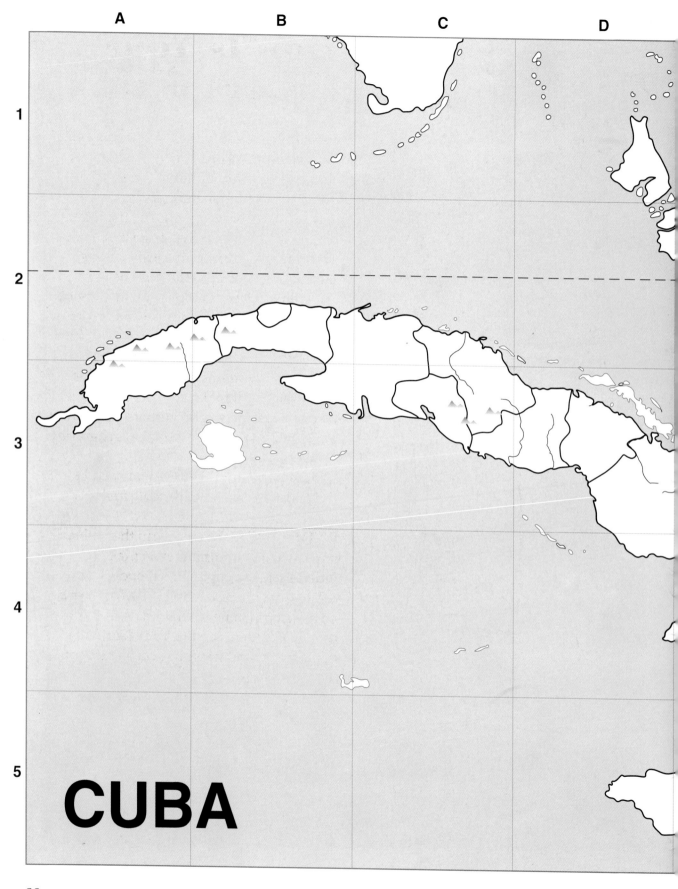

A   B   C   D

1

2

3

4

5

CUBA

88

How Is Your Geography?

Learning to identify the main geographical areas and points of a country can be challenging. Although it may seem difficult at first to memorize the locations and spellings of major cities or the names of mountain ranges, rivers, deserts, lakes, and other prominent physical features, the end result of this effort can be very rewarding. Places you previously did not know existed will suddenly come to life when referred to in world news, whether in newspapers, television reports, or other books and reference sources. This knowledge will make you feel a bit closer to the rest of the world, with its fascinating variety of cultures and physical geography.

Used in a classroom setting, the instructor can make duplicates of this map using a copy machine. (PLEASE DO NOT WRITE IN THIS BOOK!) Students can then fill in any requested information on their individual map copies. Used one-on-one, the student can also make copies of the map on a copy machine and use them as a study tool. The student can practice identifying place names and geographical features on his or her own.

Cuba at a Glance

Official Name	República de Cuba, Republic of Cuba
Capital	Havana
Official Language	Spanish
Population	11,064,000 (1998 estimate)
Land Area	42,804 square miles (110,860 square km)
Provinces	Camagüey, Ciego de Avila, Cienfuegos, Ciudad de La Habana, Granma, Guantánamo, Holguín, La Habana, Las Tunas, Matanzas, Pinar del Río, Sancti Spíritus, Santiago de Cuba, Villa Clara
Major Cities	Bayamo, Camagüey, Guantánamo, Holguín, Santiago de Cuba
Major Mountains	Sierra Maestra, Sierra de los Órganos, Sierra de Trinidad
Highest Point	Pico Turquino 6,561 feet (2,000 meters)
Major Rivers	Cauto, Sagua la Grande, Zaza
Famous Leaders	Máximo Gómez (1836–1905), José Martí (1853–1895), Fulgencio Batista (1901–1973), Ernesto "Che" Guevara (1928–1967), Fidel Castro (c. 1926–)
National Flower	Butterfly Jasmine
National Tree	Royal Palm
Major Festivals	Romería de Mayo (May), Festival of Caribbean Culture (June), Carnaval (July–August), Havana International Jazz Festival (December), Las Parrandas (December)
Major Holidays	Anniversary of the Victory of the 1959 Revolution (January 1), Anniversary of the 1895 Revolution (February 24), Anniversary of the 1953 National Rebellion (July 26)
Main Imports	Fossil fuels, food products, machinery, chemicals
Main Exports	Sugar, minerals, fish, tobacco products, citrus fruits
Currency	Cuban peso (CUP 23 = U.S. $1 as of 1999)

Opposite: **The expanding tourist industry has caused a boom in Cuban souvenir stalls.**

Glossary

Cuban Vocabulary

almácega (ahl-MAH-cey-gah): a Cuban tree that has medicinal leaves.

babalawos (bah-bah-LAHOS): Santerían priests.

balseros (bahl-SEH-rohs): Cuban emigrants who flee their country in makeshift rafts.

bolero (bo-LEH-roh): a children's game in which a player must catch a small ball inside a wooden cup.

camello (cah-MEY-yoh): "camel." A bus that has a hump-shaped cabin trailer.

campismos (cahm-PEES-mos): rural campsites for student getaways.

capa (KAH-pah): the wrapper, or outermost tobacco leaf, of a cigar.

carrozas (cah-RROH-sahs): decorative floats used in the Las Parrandas festival.

Changó (chahn-GOH): an orisha who controls fire.

comparsas (kom-PAR-sahs): dancing groups that perform during Carnaval.

congris (cohn-GREESE): a favorite Cuban dish made of rice and black beans.

cyclobus (see-cloh-BOOSE): a special public bus that transports cyclists.

El Morro (ehl MOH-roh): a Spanish-built fortress that guards Havana Bay.

guajiros (gwa-HEE-rohs): Cubans who live in the countryside.

Guantanamera (gwahn-tah-nah-MEH-rah): "woman from Guantánamo." A famous guajira song that is also the title of a film directed by Tomás Gutiérrez Alea.

jutía (hoo-TEE-ah): a tree-dwelling, ratlike mammal native to Cuba.

lechón (leh-CHONE): roast pork.

lector (lek-TORE): a hired reader who entertains cigar factory workers.

machismo (mah-CHEES-moh): an exaggerated attitude of manliness.

majá (ma-HAH): a nocturnal python found in the Zapata Marsh.

Malecón (mah-leh-CONE): a seawall guarding the outskirts of Havana.

marímbola (mah-RIM-bo-lah): a thumb piano having five metal keys.

mimosas sensitivas (mee-MOH-sahs sen-see-TEE-vahs): a Cuban plant, the leaves of which curl up after being touched.

mogotes (moh-GOH-tehs): flat-topped mountain formations found in the province of Pinar del Río.

Nueva Trova (new-AY-vah TROH-vah): "New Minstrels." A popular form of Cuban folk music.

Obatalá (oh-bah-tah-LAH): an orisha who is often associated with Jesus Christ.

orishas (oh-REE-shahs): Santerían saints.

paladares (pah-lah-DAR-ehs): small, private, family-owned restaurants.

Punto Guajiro (POON-toh gwa-HEE-roh): Cuban country music.

rumba (ROOM-bah): a vigorous music and dance style derived from son.

son (SONE): a traditional, rustic style of Cuban music featuring "call and response" vocal patterns.

tres (TREYSS): a three-stringed guitar.

Yemanyá (yeh-mahn-YAH): a female orisha who controls the seas.

yuca (YOO-cah): an edible, potato-like root.

English Vocabulary

Afro-Cuban: referring to a black Cuban who has African cultural roots.

archipelago: a chain of islands.

baroque: referring to a highly decorative artistic style popular during the seventeenth and eighteenth centuries.

capitalism: an economic system in which private individuals or companies control the production and distribution of goods and services.

colonial: referring to a relationship in which a powerful nation dictates the government and economy of a weaker nation in order to extend its cultural and political influence. Also refers to a style of architecture found in European colonies during the 1700s and 1800s.

communist: referring to a system of government in which all of a nation's wealth and property are collectively owned by its people and are distributed equally among them.

corsairs: sailors who were hired to raid Spanish ships and New World colonies.

counterrevolutionary: opposing a revolutionary movement.

creole: an American-born Spaniard.

defect: to desert one's country.

dissenter: a person who openly expresses his or her opinions in opposition to a government or political system.

embargo: a government order prohibiting commerce with another country.

exile: (n.) a person who has been banished from his or her native land.

free enterprise: the capitalist principle of letting private businesses operate without government regulation.

guerrilla warfare: the use of surprise attacks by small groups of soldiers to fight a much larger enemy force.

leftist: liberal or radical.

mestizos: people of mixed European and native American Indian ancestry.

mulatto: a person of mixed European and African ancestry.

nationalized: converted from private ownership to government ownership.

neoclassical: pertaining to a style of art, literature, or architecture that revives ancient Greek or Roman forms.

occupation: the act of controlling a foreign territory by sending military forces into it.

organic agriculture: a method of farming that uses fertilizers and pesticides developed from natural organisms instead of synthetic chemicals.

pesticides: chemical-based agents that eliminate insects which destroy agricultural crops.

phonetics: the range of sounds within a particular language.

rationing: a method of distributing scarce resources equally among the population.

Santería: an Afro-Cuban religion that incorporates elements of Catholicism in the worship of African deities.

satire: a literary or artistic work that uses irony or sarcasm to ridicule its subjects.

socialism: a political system in which the government owns and controls the means of a nation's economy.

spelunking: exploring caves.

sustainable agriculture: a method of farming that renourishes the soil so crops can be grown on the same land indefinitely.

More Books to Read

Cars of Cuba. Cristina Garcia and Joshua Greene (Harry N. Abrams)

Cuba. Countries of the World series. William P. Mara (Bridgestone Books)

Cuba. Cultures of the World series. Sean Sheehan (Benchmark Books)

Cuba in Pictures. Nathan A. Haverstock (Lerner)

The Cuban American Family Album. American Family Albums series. Dorothy and Thomas Hoobler (Oxford University Press)

Cuban Women Confront the Future: Three Decades After the Revolution. Vilma Espin Guillois (Ocean Press)

Culture Shock! Cuba. Culture Shock! series. Mark Cramer (Graphic Arts Center)

Old Havana, Cuba. Travel to Landmarks series. Nicolas Sapieha and Francesco Venturi (I. B. Tauris & Co., Ltd.)

The Reader's Companion to Cuba. Alan Ryan and Christa Malone, editors (Harcourt Brace)

Videos

Cuba: Island of Dreams. (Ivn Entertainment)

I Am Cuba. (Milestone Films)

Island Time Warp: Trains in Cuba. (Canadian Caboose Press)

Roots of Rhythm. (New Video Groups)

Web Sites

www.zpub.com/cpp

www.salsaweb.com

www.cubanet.org

pangaea.org/cuba_natural_history_nature/cuba.htm

Due to the dynamic nature of the Internet, some web sites stay current longer than others. To find additional web sites, use a reliable search engine with one or more of the following keywords to help you locate information about Cuba. Keywords: *Fidel Castro, cigars, Ernesto "Che" Guevara, Havana, rumba, salsa, Santería, Santiago de Cuba, son.*

Index